BREAK
New Ground
WITH GOD

How the Transfiguration Of Jesus Can
Re-Energize Your Faith

David Squyres

Copyright © 2017 by David Squyres

All rights reserved. This book or any portion thereof may not be reproduced in any manner whatsoever without the express written permission of the publisher except for the use of brief quotations in a book review.

Printed in the United States of America

Cover art design by Lynette Bonner

First edition published August 15, 2017

18 17   1 2

Squyres, David

Break New Ground with God / David Squyres

p. cm.

ISBN-13: 978-1548260637
ISBN-10: 1548260630

This paper meets the requirements of ANSI/NISO Z39.48-1992 (Permanence of Paper)

Unless otherwise noted, all scripture quotes are from the NIV (New International Version), Copyright © 1973, 1978, 1984 by International Bible Society.

Dedication

For Susie Karyn Squyres

Also known as Susie Paloosie and Susie the Superstar, who brings joy, laughter and heavy doses of insanity to our home. May the God of Heaven grace you with a faith that will endure to the end.

Acknowledgements

First, I would like to thank my wife, Rebecca, who is a wellspring of joy in my life. Her happiness and simple faith in Jesus has strengthened my walk with the Lord.

And a word of love to my earthly father, Dewey F. Squyres, who taught me from childhood what it meant to love the Lord and follow him. He not only gave me a bedrock of right doctrine, he showed me Christianity by living what he believed even when it cost him.

No large project is done alone. I would like to express my sincere thanks to Mr. Jim Wilson, who edited and formatted the manuscript. Jim helped me think through every aspect of this book. The journey together was spiritually invigorating and refreshing to me. Some people come into your life and bless you over and over again; Jim and his wife Loretta have done exactly that in my life.

Thanks to a couple of women who added tremendously to this book. First, to Susan Davis, who helped generate questions in the Digging Deeper section. And second to Donna McDowell, who read early drafts and offered enthusiastic encouragement. These ladies are the kind of church member every pastor wants because they make the church a sweeter place.

Finally, I would like to thank the unique and all together beautiful congregation of Palms Baptist Church. They have been a great joy to me throughout my years as their pastor. Rebecca and I have not only felt their love for us, but more importantly their love for Jesus. Walking together as a church family is a special experience, and we are glad for the years our footprints traveled God's path side by side.

Six Truths for *Breaking New Ground with God*

As we study the Bible, the Transfiguration and discuss ways to *Break New Ground with God*, these six truths will be at the center of our conversation.

1	Prayer is the true source of a believer's guidance and power
2	A personal sense of awe and wonder is vital to spiritual growth
3	The Second Coming is a real event that we live toward
4	God's Word must be read for truth, not just comfort
5	The Lord deeply cares about personal suffering
6	Faithfulness in the face of hardship will be greatly rewarded

Table of Contents

1. It's Time To Break New Ground 1
2. Ascending The Mountain 13
3. Jesus' Secret—Truth #1 27
4. Put The Awe Back In Awesome—Truth #2 41
5. Transforming Power Of The Second Coming—Truth #3 57
6. Why Listening To Jesus Is Painful—Truth #4 75
7. Rethink How You Read The Bible 87
8. New Ground With Your Emotions—Truth #5 99
9. What You Have To Drop To Finish Well—Truth #6 119
10. Building On New Ground 133

1 It's Time To Break New Ground

> *Sow for yourselves righteousness, reap the fruit of unfailing love, and break up your unplowed ground; for it is time to seek Yahweh.*
> Hosea 10:12

Have you been stuck in your walk with God? Is it time to dig a little deeper? Is it time to begin moving beyond cultural Christianity and really follow Jesus? For each of us, we must decide: do we want to stay comfortable, or break new ground with God?

To break new ground with God means to get past clichés and easy answers, and move to unfamiliar ground. It means that while we maintain age old spiritual habits, we engage them in a new way. Instead of simply seeking comfort from God's Word, we seek truth from the Bible. Instead of going to God and making a series of demands of him in prayer, we change how we see prayer and engage with God in a constant conversation that allows him to direct our every move.

Breaking new ground with God is not easy. We get stuck in spiritual ruts. We get stuck in emotional pits. We get tired and sometimes we're not even sure it's worth the effort. But it is!

If you picked this book up and read the title, *Break New Ground with God*, I hope something in your heart stirred. I hope you thought, "Yes! That's what I need!"

Breaking New Ground with God Takes Faith

A young man breathes a quiet prayer as he stares down into a hole in the earth. Somewhere, from deep inside the caverns, he can hear the low growl of lions. Daniel looks at the king and then back to the hole.

Break New Ground With God

The lions can smell him and are beginning to gather at the mouth of the cave awaiting his descent. *"I shall fear no evil, for thou art with me,"* he prays quietly. He is surprised at his own resolve and excited at the faith he feels boiling inside him. He holds back a smile, not wanting to be cocky, and nods to the king. Then he descends into the pit.

The wind drives against his desert chafed skin. He stares into the darkness at the sea—behind him he can hear the roar of the nation as they cry out in panic. Pharaoh's army is nearby, separated only by a strange cloud that threatens to lift any moment. Moses wants to argue with God about the wisdom of his plan, but finally lifts his staff with steady determination over the water. He believed God wouldn't fail him, but the sound of the water whipping up into the air and splitting in two still surprises him. It moves with such force he is left wiping saltwater from his eyes.

A woman carefully tears her only red dress until she has a long strip of scarlet. The dye that made that beautiful dress cost her greatly, but she is ready to give up everything. Going to the window she looks down on the strange people marching below. A gold box leads them as they move with eager anticipation; something great is about to happen. Hearing of these people once made Rahab tremble with fear, but this was a strange way to win a war. Just marching around a wall? She realizes she doesn't have much time—they are on their seventh pass around the wall. She secures her strip of scarlet in the window as trumpets blast down below, followed by a shout. The ground below her begins to quake. She can hear the steady thunder of the city wall collapsing on itself. For a moment fear grips her. Her house is part of the wall. Will the God she has just put her faith in now let her down? She runs her hand against the scarlet cord in her window—she will trust the Lord. It takes a moment for her to realize the devastation has ended. Dust is thick in the air as she looks around. Her house is still standing.

We all love stories of faith. True stories. We respect men and women who walked in God's power and did not fear. When I read about Moses, David, Daniel, Joshua, Rahab and an unnamed Centurion I am left gasping, "Lord! I want faith like that!"

When I see people of faith, people who can look into a lion's den or call for the sun to stand still in the sky, I am left realizing just how far my own faith has to go.

Chapter 1—It's Time To Break New Ground

Before I can look into a lion's den and not fear, or face off against a giant, or trust God to hold my house up when the entire city wall is falling down—my faith needs to increase.

It was faith that caused Peter to step onto the water. It was faith that drove Abraham as he prepared to sacrifice his only son on the mountain. It was faith that led the early church to pray all night until a startled apostle appeared on their doorstep—freed from prison by an angel of God.

It was faith that moved Peter and John to tell the religious leaders of their day, *"You decide if we should obey you or God. But we can't keep it in! We've seen things too wonderful to keep silent now."*

These had what we call faith. Faith for them was not a magic word or a wistful hope; it was a dynamic, growing, intimate relationship with God. Here's the amazing thing—a relationship with the same God is offered to us. Does it ever excite you that we know the God who Joshua prayed to? That boggles my mind. And we are invited into a love relationship with him.

Spiritual life, like any deep relationship, takes maintenance. It requires work to really know, love and walk with God. Raw passion can't do it. Passion, like fuel that burns bright on a fire can flare up for a season, but it cannot sustain a lifetime. Passion can come in steady, wonderful seasons, but a personal relationship is what really carries us through.

Faith is the thing we will come back to time and again as we seek to break new ground with God. To change how you read the Bible or how you pray will require faith. To change old habits and really follow Christ will take faith. And God loves faith!

Breaking New Ground with God Takes Desire

The prophet Hosea wrote:

> *Sow for yourselves righteousness, reap the fruit of unfailing love, and break up your unplowed ground; for it is time to seek Yahweh.*
>
> — Hosea 10:12

Hosea is telling us that we can have a great breakthrough with God. We can actually have victory over our sins by living a righteous life. We can enjoy resting in true love, free from worry and fear. It's there for the taking, but we must do something. The prophet demands we *break up* the unplowed ground. Our hearts are like soil that can easily get hard over time. Enough rain beating down, followed by months of sunlight, and the ground starts to harden. Go through a few storms followed by droughts, and over time if you're not careful your heart starts to get hard and cynical.

Hosea gives us a nudge—it's time to seek the Lord. No more wasting time. No more thinking one day we'll change our behavior. Life is slipping away, and with it our opportunity to really live for God.

If we really want a breakthrough with God, it takes a desire on our part. We have to want to bad enough to make the changes necessary to actually walk further with God than we have so far.

A few years ago, my family decided to plant pumpkins. They all died. Everyone in the family was very sad. We later tried to plant watermelon. They also died! Nothing would grow in that spot. What is it about that one spot in our yard? Why would nothing grow? One day in frustration I started digging and quickly discovered the problem—a slab of cement was buried there. I began to clear the slab wondering how big it was. It was BIG!

My wife came out and in her wisdom said, "That's not cement, it's hard dirt."

"No, look," I said, scraping it clean, "it's cement."

I then took my shovel and hit the ground very hard. Nothing happened. Three more strikes and suddenly the ground opened. Under that hard patch of dirt, I'd thought was cement, was soft ground that we could plant in. We just had to break through the hard ground. I later learned the type of dirt is called *caliche*. You could build a fort on it!

Some people are happy with shallowness. They don't need to dig down deep or seek more from God. They don't need breakthroughs. For them, a ticket into Heaven is enough. Just so long as they get in the door of Heaven, that's all they want from God, assurance that the future is taken care of so they can enjoy the now. That's not at all what it means to follow Jesus, and I'll bet that's not you—is it?

I'll bet you're reading this book because something in you desires to go deeper with God. Even if it's painful—even if it takes work—you're ready.

Chapter 1—It's Time To Break New Ground

Six Truths for *Breaking New Ground with God*

1	Prayer is the true source of a believer's guidance and power
2	A personal sense of awe and wonder is vital to spiritual growth
3	The Second Coming is a real event that we live toward
4	God's Word must be read for truth, not just comfort
5	The Lord deeply cares about personal suffering
6	Faithfulness in the face of hardship will be greatly rewarded

What Happens when you Break New Ground with God

To break new ground with God is to experience God in a new way. It is to have a breakthrough in your faith or understanding of God. It is choosing to be obedient in an area of your life you have previously displayed stubbornness. When we have a breakthrough with God, the results can be monumental—life changing.

Often a breakthrough with God accompanies our spiritual eyes being opened. We see new things that we had been blind to. There are a whole lot of things we can't see with our eyes—gravity, magnetism, radio waves, light waves. There are even some colors we can't see. There are some things only God sees. In fact, there is a whole spirit world with angels, demons, and more that we don't naturally see. But sometimes a spiritual breakthrough is accompanied by spiritual sight in an area. You may not see angels or demons, but God might open your eyes in a new way to a situation you're going through. God may show you someone suffering that you previously overlooked. I think it's very likely God will open your eyes to what he is doing in a situation so that you can be a part of it. Jesus often called his disciples to—*Follow me*. In other words, let me show you what I'm doing so you can be part of it.

Another thing that happens when we experience a spiritual breakthrough is we become disturbed. That was probably unexpected, right? But, if our eyes are closed tight and we are focused on ourselves, we tend to not be bothered by the things that bother God. When our spiritual eyes are opened, when we encounter God in a new way, our hearts become very responsive to the things that concern him. You may have never cared about the poor, until you came a step closer to God, and he began to disturb you. You may have broken new ground in reading your Bible, but as you did so, you also became disturbed at how many people around you are truly lost and headed for hell. Be ready, if you want to break new ground with God, you are going to be disturbed and your life will be disrupted. You cannot encounter God in new ways and remain the same.

We can also expect that our own hearts will be refreshed as we break new ground with God. We will experience joy from the Holy Spirit as we step closer to the Lord and begin to do his will.

When we break new ground with God, our appetite is wetted and we begin to want more. Our spiritual hunger is increased, and one breakthrough can quickly lead to another. As you begin reading your Bible more, your joy increases and you are convicted that you also need to become a person of prayer. Soon, as you take on the habit of prayer and find many breakthroughs in your prayer life, you sense God telling you to serve in your church. Maybe you've never served God before, but suddenly you are hungry to give yourself to a cause bigger than you. Seeking to break new ground with God is not a one-step journey where a single breakthrough will get you where you want to be. Instead, our journey with God will be defined by many breakthroughs.

The Transfiguration and your Walk with God

In the journey through this book, the Transfiguration will be our north star. The events that unfolded on the Mount of Transfiguration transformed the disciples and has the potential to radically help believers today move forward with God.

The story of the Transfiguration is recorded in all four Gospels, and is also mentioned by the Apostle Peter. When we think of great moments in the life of Jesus, we tend to think of miracles like the feeding of the five thousand, or Jesus walking on water, or raising Lazarus from the dead. Ask a fellow believer their favorite miracle of

Jesus', and they are sure to mention the calming of the storm, the resurrection of Lazarus—and certainly let's not forget the time he spit on the ground and rubbed mud in a blind man's eyes! All good stuff. But what about the Transfiguration? "Oh yeah, that one, too," some are sure to agree, as if reminded of an incidental miracle on a list.

The Transfiguration is much more than just *one more* miracle. In the Transfiguration, God lays out a dynamic path for a deeper relationship with Jesus. It was there, on the mountain top as Jesus glowed with God's glory, that the Lord made it clear that Jesus was not just an ordinary person. And this is no ordinary story.

Basic Habits of our Christian Walk Found in the Story of the Transfiguration

- **Prayer**—Jesus was praying.
- **Bible reading**—Moses and Elijah represent the Scriptures—law and prophets.
- **Time alone with God**—Jesus took a group of disciples to be alone with him.
- **Importance of listening to Jesus**—The voice from Heaven commands them to listen.
- **Correction**—Peter spoke out of turn and was corrected.
- **Inspirational worship**—God exalts Jesus to a place of worship.

We need all six of these habits daily. We need time alone with God in prayer and in his Word. Time spent listening to him and allowing him to correct us. And that special time each day is a time given to worshiping God and putting him first.

The phrase to *break new ground* is the idea of doing something completely different from how it's been done before. In the pages ahead, we will look at how we can engage the spiritual disciplines like Scripture reading and prayer in fresh ways. How can we experience newness in our walk with God? For many of us, we must change our approach to some of the basic spiritual habits.

Rugged faith, the kind that can really go the distance, must be maintained. Like any relationship, our relationship with God requires constant attention.

Maybe you've been through some rough valleys this last year. Maybe you've had some losses that really took the wind out of you—not only physically, but spiritually. Maybe it was the death of a loved one, or the loss of a relationship, or job, or friendship. Maybe you got busy and neglected your walk with the Lord, and now the emptiness is becoming a great hollow void.

Whatever the reason, you feel the Holy Spirit nudging you; it's time to come back. Time to return to the fire, the zeal, the joy of the faith. Come on, I can't wait to show you this incredible story.

Digging Deeper

1. What do you envision when you think of breaking new ground with God?

   _____
   _____
   _____

2. If you are seeking to break new ground with God, think honestly over these questions:

   - What is your greatest distraction to seeking God?

     _____
     _____
     _____
     _____

   - How aware are you of the places where your heart has become hard toward God?

     _____
     _____
     _____
     _____

   - Are you willing to allow God to disturb you, or do you want to stay comfortable?

     _____
     _____
     _____
     _____

3. Toward the end of the chapter, there were some spiritual disciplines identified. Which of these do you think God would ask you to become more committed to in the coming days?
    - [ ] Prayer
    - [ ] Bible reading
    - [ ] Time alone with God
    - [ ] Importance of listening to Jesus
    - [ ] Correction
    - [ ] Inspirational Worship

4. What do you want more than a relationship with God?

    _____
    _____
    _____
    _____

    What holds you back?

    _____
    _____
    _____
    _____

5. Take a moment and read the story of the Transfiguration (Matthew 17:1-13, Mark 9:2-13, Luke 9:28-36). Write down some of the details that stand out to you.

    _____
    _____
    _____
    _____

Chapter 1—It's Time To Break New Ground

6. The six truths identified at the beginning of this study are central to our study. Review them and put a X by the ones that best identifies an area where you need to breakthrough with God.

    - [ ] Prayer is the true source of a believer's guidance and power.
    - [ ] A personal sense of Awe and wonder is vital to spiritual health.
    - [ ] The Second Coming is a real event that we live toward.
    - [ ] God's Word must be read for truth, not just comfort.
    - [ ] The Lord deeply cares about our personal suffering.
    - [ ] Faithfulness in the face of hardship will be greatly rewarded.

7. What is faith to you?

    _____
    _____
    _____
    _____

    Do you see it as a feeling or what you do?

    _____
    _____
    _____
    _____

2 Ascending The Mountain

Jesus took with him Peter, James and John the brother of James, and led them up a high mountain by themselves. There he was transfigured before them. His face shone like the sun, and his clothes became as white as the light. Just then there appeared before them Moses and Elijah, talking with Jesus. Matthew 17:1-2

Jesus took Peter, and the brothers James and John up on a high mountain where they could be alone. The traditional site for this event is Mount Tabor, an 1,886-foot mountain that overlooks the Jezreel Valley. In the valley is Megiddo, where the book of Revelation pictures the armies of the earth coming to fight.

As Jesus was praying, an unbelievable miracle took place. The appearance of Jesus' face and clothes changed. Mark says in amazement that his clothes became radiant white—so white, he insists, that no one on planet earth could have bleached them that color. Mark wants to be sure we understand that Jesus didn't just give his clothes a good washing before going up the mountain. Luke goes even further, stating that Jesus' garments became as bright as a flash of lightning. On a dark stormy night, a flash of lightning can transform the sky. You can't miss it. In this instance, Jesus' very garments were so bright they could have lit the night sky. Like Mark, Luke is emphatic that this isn't something that could be faked. There is no way to make clothes so bright they shine like lightning—even if you're a rock star.

Matthew describes Jesus' face, saying that it shone like the sun. While lightning might flash for a moment with glistening light, the sun beams with steady radiant illumination. It is reminiscent of the way Moses' face glowed when he came down Mount Sinai with the

Ten Commandments in his hands. But in Moses' case, the illumination was hidden when they clothed or veiled his face. Not so with Jesus. What happened to Jesus was so powerful, even his clothing shined. It's like his presence burned right through his clothes. In fact, we are told that his clothes were *exastrapto,* that is, *radiant.*

Standing with the Departed

As Jesus' appearance changed, another astonishing thing happened. Two men who had been central characters in the Old Testament appeared—Moses and Elijah. The Greek says they appeared *doxa,* or *in glory.* That is, their appearance was also amazing. But don't get stuck on their appearance—think about this—Moses and Elijah appeared! That would cause your jaw to drop in utter disbelief for a couple of reasons.

First, Moses and Elijah had both been long gone from planet earth. Further, Moses and Elijah themselves were not contemporaries. Moses lead Israel during the time of the Exodus, and Elijah was a prophet during the Divided Kingdom. They were separated by about 600 years. That would be like George Washington and Franklin Roosevelt appearing together—only they are separated by a much smaller time gap. Elijah once ran to Mount Sinai in an hour of desperation, as if to take refuge in the place where God had given the Law. But he did not personally know Moses until he arrived in Heaven in a whirlwind. These are two men who stand on almost opposite ends of the Old Testament. We often think of Moses as representing the Law (the Torah) and of Elijah as representing the Prophets.

Second, not only did Moses and Elijah show up, but they began talking to the Messiah. While any of us would be excited to talk to Jesus face to face today, for the apostles that was a daily experience. Jesus was very ordinary to them. Initially, they saw something extraordinary happen to his body; then people they knew only from the Scriptures showed up and began talking to their glowing leader!

Eavesdropping at the Transfiguration

Did you know that several times the Bible allows us to eavesdrop on the Trinity? For instance in Hebrews 10 we read the prayer God the Son spoke to God the Father as he became incarnate. Psalm 110 is a letter written from God the Father to God the Son. Imagine reading the Bible and finding a letter written directly to you in it. No wonder it's the most quoted Psalm in all the New Testament. At the transfiguration, we are allowed to do a smidgen of eavesdropping. In this case, we are not listening in on the Trinity, but on a conversation between Moses, Elijah, and Jesus.

So what were they talking about? Luke 9:31 provides some clues on their conversation when it states that the three *"spoke of his departure, which he was about to accomplish at Jerusalem"* (ESV).

They were talking about his death in Jerusalem—his death on the cross. What a fantastic conversation with three incredible men. Moses, Elijah, and Jesus stood on the mountain—all glowing—and discussed the crucifixion of Jesus.

Did the two visitors come bearing a message? Did they want to encourage him? The details of the discussion are not provided, so it's not for us to know. What was said was between them. Hopefully in Heaven we can check out a Blu-ray disc.

It is interesting that most translations say they were discussing his *departure* which was going to happen in Jerusalem. Departure is more literally translated *exodus*.

That they were speaking of his *exodus* suggests more than just his death on the cross. In many ways Jesus' death would mirror the Hebrew exodus. Jesus was the Passover Lamb and his death would set us free from the slavery of sin. But that's not at all the end of the story. The Exodus refers not only to the Passover, but the full escape from Egypt through the Red Sea and to freedom. Jesus not only sacrificed his life, but he crossed over from death to life. The picture of the Exodus should remind us of the full scope of Christ work—his death, burial, and resurrection. Moses and Elijah were not just discussing with Jesus his sacrifice on Calvary, but his victory over death at the resurrection.

Before Jesus went down the mountain and began final preparations to head for the cross, he had a discussion with Moses. Moses, the one who stood before Pharaoh and called down plagues on Egypt. He talked to the prophet who parted the sea and lead the people on a great journey toward the Promised Land. But Moses was unable to complete the mission. He may have liberated them from slavery, but he could not liberate them from their own self-inflicted bondage. Under Moses' leadership, the Hebrews refused to enter the Promised Land and died in the wilderness. Jesus, unlike Moses, would set us free from the bondage of sin and bring us into the Promised Land.

Peter was excited by what was happening right in front of him. Never short on ideas, the apostle declared that what they needed were three tents, one for Moses, one for Elijah, and one for Jesus. Peter certainly meant to honor Jesus—he was putting Jesus equal to Elijah and their most revered prophet, Moses. He felt this was an occasion that should be marked. The site itself ought to be a place people could return to. But Luke tells us plainly that Peter did not know what he was talking about. God's intent was not to put Jesus on par with Moses and Elijah, but to highly exalt him above Moses and Elijah. And, God certainly did not need three tents for future pilgrimages to the site of the transfiguration.

I once saw a preacher on TV standing outside the traditional tomb of Jesus. He made a big deal of going inside, and after a moment he came out grinning. "I can still feel a little of that resurrection power!" he exclaimed. Frankly, I'm not buying it. God's power doesn't linger around in a place like static electricity. God wasn't excited about monuments two thousand years ago, and he's not excited about them now. God wants us more focused on the person of Jesus than the place of events. God didn't need three tents to service future pilgrims who might be seeking a little jolt of Transfiguration power. God wanted them to learn something about Jesus.

So, God interrupted Peter.

Pause on that for a moment. God himself had to interrupt Peter. Of course, Peter was apparently interrupting Jesus' conversation with Moses and Elijah. Peter was so focused on how they might mark the occasion that he was not even fully present.

How Did Peter Know Moses and Elijah?

It's interesting that Peter was able to recognize Moses and Elijah without any introductions. Peter had never met either of these two great prophets, so how did he recognize them? Some scholars suggest that perhaps they were each holding something that would identify them. Moses holding the Ten Commandments and Elijah a staff. A better answer is that the Heavenly body is immediately recognizable. Maybe we won't need name tags in Heaven; we will immediately identify one another just as quickly as Peter knew he was looking at Moses and Elijah.

The Garment of His Glory

While Peter was still talking, Matthew tells us that a *bright* cloud came over the mountain and swallowed them up. A bright cloud, bright clothes—all of it has an other-worldly sense.

Several times in the Bible God's presence is shrouded in a cloud. The book of Exodus tells us that during the day a cloud led them during their wilderness journey (Exodus 13:21). Many times, in Exodus, God's presence comes down on the Tent of Meeting in the form of a cloud. A cloud that would provide shade in the intense heat of the desert. At night, the Hebrews were visited by a pillar of fire. A fire that would provide warmth for the cold desert night. Throughout the Bible the cloud often serves as a symbol of God's glory.

References of a Cloud as a Symbol of God's Glory

[T]he whole Israelite community, they looked toward the desert, and there was the glory of Yahweh appearing in the cloud. (Exodus 16:10)

Then the cloud covered the Tent of Meeting, and the glory of Yahweh filled the tabernacle. Moses could not enter the Tent of Meeting because the cloud had settled upon it, and the glory of Yahweh filled the tabernacle. (Exodus 40:34-35)

He makes the clouds his chariot and rides on the wings of the wind. (Psalm 104:3)

There is no one like the God of Jeshurun, who rides on the Heavens to help you and on the clouds in his majesty. (Deuteronomy 33:26)

When Jesus ascended back into Heaven, he went up into a cloud. Noted theologian, F.F. Bruce writes in his commentary on Acts:

> The cloud in each case (the Transfiguration and the Ascension) is probably to be interpreted as the cloud of the Shekinah—the cloud which resting above the tent of meeting in the days of Moses, was the visible token to Israel that the glory of the Lord dwelt within. So, at the last moment that the apostles saw their Lord with outward vision, they were granted a theophany: Jesus is enveloped in the cloud of the divine presence.

It's like the cloud serves like a garment for God's glory on earth. It protects human eyes from staring into the Shekinah.

The cloud not only appeared in the past, but we will see it again. Jesus said he would come back on the clouds. When asked directly by the High Priest if he was the Christ, Jesus did not mince words. He said, "*I am*" and then told the High Priest he would see him coming at the right hand of the Mighty One coming on the clouds of Heaven (see Mark 14:62).

On the mountain with Peter, James, John, Moses, Elijah, and Jesus—now appears a cloud. And from the cloud, from *his chariot* (see Psalm 104:3), God is going to speak.

As the cloud engulfed them, Luke tells us that they were afraid. They had not been afraid, but excited at the appearance of Jesus. Even his radical change did not inspire fear so much as joy. But this cloud was a terrifying thing. It is as if they are aware that the Presence of the Almighty is now on the mountain in an unusual way and holy fear gripped the disciples.

Three Times the Father Spoke During the Ministry of Jesus

Any time God speaks directly into human history is an amazing moment. In fact, God only spoke from heaven three times during the ministry of Jesus. It's worth taking a moment to look at those three times.

First, God spoke when Jesus was baptized to display his approval of the Son at the beginning of Jesus' ministry. Talk about an incredible moment—think about what happened at Jesus' baptism. The Prophet John baptized the Son of God. The Spirit of God descended in the form of a dove and God the Father declared that he was *pleased* with Jesus. God openly and verbally gave his approval for the work, ministry, and person of Jesus.

While there were many people who came claiming to represent God, the Father himself made it clear that Jesus was his true representative on earth. No other prophet has had God validate their ministry the way the Father validated the Messiah's work right at the beginning of his ministry.

Note the importance of Jesus' baptism in terms of Trinitarian doctrine. Modalism is the idea that God the Father became the son and later became the Spirit. But at the baptism of Jesus, all three were present at the same time carrying out unique roles.

The second time God the Father's voice spoke during the life of Jesus was on the mount of transfiguration. The voice came from the cloud and declared, *"This is my Son, my Chosen One; listen to him!"* (Luke 9:35, ESV). *Chosen one* could be *beloved*. Meaning the voice may have said, *"This is the son I love, listen to him."*

In those moments, God interrupted Peter's monologue about building monuments and told the disciples to *listen to Jesus.*

The third time God the Father spoke during the ministry of Jesus was close to Jesus' death (Jesus called it his *hour*). John 12 tells us that a voice from heaven spoke and God the Father said that he had glorified his name in the life of Jesus, and that he would glorify it again (see John 12:28). That is, Jesus glorified God in both the life he lived and in his sacrificial death.

The scene in John 12 gives us a brief perspective on the voice of God. While some in the crowd heard the words God spoke, others were sure it had been the roar of thunder. Now, thunder in the distance is cool, but up close it can shake entire structures and knock grown men to the ground.

Each time God spoke, he was communicating something very important he wanted us to know about his son Jesus. Let's focus in on what God said about Jesus at the transfiguration.

Exalted Over Everything

By calling Jesus his Son, God the Father clarified Jesus' unique position in the universe. He's not equal to Moses and Elijah—he is superior. The unique title of Sonship belongs solely to the Second Person of the Trinity—Jesus.

This is a reference from Psalm 2:

> The LORD said to me, 'You are my Son. Today I have begotten you.'
>
> — Psalm 2:7, ESV

It's as if God on the mountain says, *"Well, I told you long ago He was coming. Now here He is!"* This is more than a declaration of Jesus as Messiah. This expresses his unequaled relationship within the confines of the Trinity itself.

The theme of Jesus' unique position as the Son of God resounds through the book of Hebrews. It is most simply to say this—*There is no one else like Jesus.* He is unique and above all creation. While he stands outside creation as Creator, he entered into our creation and became flesh.

At the Transfiguration, as the Son glowed, the Father acknowledged before human witnesses that Jesus is exalted above everything. Think about who God said this to. Standing there were five humans; three living apostles, and two making an earthly visit from Heaven. Before them, God declared that Jesus is not an ordinary man, but the Son of God. He has a unique relationship to the Father in which he is co-equal but chose to submit to the Father.

Hebrews 1:5 quotes Psalm 2, pointing out that God never called any of the angels his *Son*. Because Son of God is not a title an angel can carry. Only Jesus can be fully realized as the Son of God. It is in his position as Son of God that he brings us into relationship with the Father, making us children of God.

Lord Timothy Dexter
(1748-1806)

Lord Timothy Dexter was an idiot. Really. He made his fortune buying boat loads of Continental currency during the Revolutionary War. At the time, their value was sinking and it was thought they would soon be worthless, so people were glad to get pennies on the dollar. Lord Dexter risked his entire savings on this venture. Fortunately for him, when the Constitution was ratified, Alexander Hamilton decided that the United States would buy back the Continentals at face value. This was a windfall for Lord Dexter! He used the money he made to buy ships and sell things all over the world. Actually, he sold junk. He was like the *Oriental Trading Company* of his day. He sold mittens in the Bahamas and collected stray cats to sell in the Caribbean islands.

Dexter wrote his life story in an autobiography titled, *A Pickle for the Knowing Ones or Plain Truth in a Homespun Dress.* He frustrated readers by refusing to use standard punctuation and seemingly random capitalization.

Lord Dexter did not get along with his wife. He married a woman much more socially affluent than he and he was sure she resented him—which she did. To prove she did not love him, he faked his own death. Three thousand people attended his wake. When he revealed he wasn't dead, he accused his wife of not mourning enough.

And here's the great part: Lord Timothy Dexter was Lord of nothing, nada, zip. He just decided to call himself Lord, thinking it would give him social standing.

Jesus is Lord not because it's a title he adopted; Jesus is Lord because he actually is the sovereign king of the universe. To confirm Jesus' preeminent standing above all creation, the voice of God the Father bursts through the Heavens and declares that this is his Son.

Jesus is not the Son of God and Lord of all because the apostles or church fathers or even the prophets decided Jesus should be. The Father from Heaven spoke into time and space to human ears to declare: THIS IS MY SON. It is not a title humans gave him, it is a title that indicates who he is.

The Apostle Paul wrote in his letter to the Philippians that:

> *[A]t the name of Jesus every knee should bow,*
>   *in Heaven and on earth and under the earth,*
> *and every tongue confess that Jesus Christ is Lord,*
>   *to the glory of God the Father.*
>
>   — Philippians 2:10-11

The true Lord is God's Son, Jesus.

Don't Tell Anyone

As they came down the mountain, were the disciples chatty or quiet? Did they pepper Jesus with questions, or were they held in spellbound silence? Probably the latter. They had just stood in the presence of Moses and Elijah and seen Jesus glorified—all that before a cloud containing the glory of the Almighty rolled by. Surely there were lumps in their throats and their knees were still a bit shaky as they tried to gather themselves.

Jesus gave them another command. He instructed them not to tell anyone what they had seen until after the resurrection. It's interesting they are not to tell until after the resurrection. It would be two of the three, Peter and John, who would be the first male disciples to discover the tomb empty. At that time, though, the three disciples had no idea what the *resurrection* was.

The Transfiguration was more than a miracle, it was a very clear demonstration of Jesus' deity. Jesus meant for this to be a private viewing for these three men, not something to be talked about around the campfire. Jesus had handpicked these three to experience this with him. Heaven had just come down on that mountain, and they had been part of it. At just the right time, God would allow them to tell others.

In his commentary, the *Jewish New Testament Commentary*, David Stern hypothesizes that because the Transfiguration confirmed Jesus' deity; it would have raised more questions than it would have answered if shared before the resurrection. Jesus' intent was not to stir confusion among his followers.

The Apostle John would write in his gospel that he had beheld Jesus glory (see John 1:14). That is, the Word not only became flesh, but the Word was more than flesh—and John himself bore witness in his Gospel that the Word was full of Glory.

Four Specific Wonders Occurred on the Mountain

1. The appearance of Jesus was transformed and became glorious.
2. The Old Testament prophets Elijah and Moses appeared with Jesus. Pretty good evidence of life after death!
3. God's voice thundered from Heaven.
4. I count the appearance of the cloud as a wonder. Generally, clouds on their own are not wondrous. However, this cloud is unusual in the timing of its arrival.

Why Did Jesus Take Them with Him?

It was certainly a special time for them as they got some more one-on-one time with the Master. Mark 9:2 notes that they were *alone*. Wouldn't you like to actually get some face-time like that with Jesus? Imagine how great it would feel if Jesus chose you and just two others to go on a spiritual retreat with him. Jesus often went alone to pray, so this extended time on the mountain was special.

The three Jesus chose made up the inner core of his followers. Peter and John would become the key leaders in the early church, along with Jesus' brother James. (The James in the Transfiguration narrative is the Apostle James, not James brother of Jesus.) All three of these men would suffer great persecution for their faith.

He took them up the mountain with him because he wanted their faith to experience a breakthrough. He would instruct them not to tell the others until after the resurrection—but his key leaders needed to see this. And don't think this is only about seeing the glory of Jesus; this was a time of prayer and teaching. Jesus wanted them to move forward in their faith and to be prepared for the events that were about to unfold in Jerusalem. He took them up the mountain because he wanted them to break some new ground with him. Don't you think they did? They did not come down the mountain the same.

God has uniquely designed the experiences and events of your life to direct your faith. He has allowed some problems, heartaches and victories to shape you into the person he wants you to be. But you're not there yet. God wants to deepen your faith. He wants to make your walk with him stronger. For that to happen, you're going to have to break new ground.

Break New Ground With God

Digging Deeper

1. Why do you think Jesus chose Peter, James, and John to go on the mountain with him?

   _____
   _____
   _____
   _____

2. Jesus told his disciples not to talk about what they had seen until after the resurrection. Why do you think he wanted them to wait?

   _____
   _____
   _____
   _____

3. Looking back, what experiences have developed your faith?

   _____
   _____
   _____
   _____

4. Have you experienced the presence of God?

   [ ] Yes   [ ] No

   What was your response?

   _____
   _____
   _____

5. What enslaves you?

    _____
    _____
    _____
    _____

    Do you see Jesus leading you to freedom?
       [ ] Yes   [ ] No

6. What does the Lordship of Jesus Christ mean to your life?

    _____
    _____
    _____
    _____

3 Jesus' Secret

Your attitude should be the same as that of Christ Jesus: Who, being in very nature God, did not consider equality with God something to be grasped, but made himself nothing, taking the very nature of a servant, being made in human likeness. And being found in appearance as a man, he humbled himself and became obedient to death—even death on a cross!

Philippians 2:5-8

What I'm about to share with you is very important both to understanding the Transfiguration and to your understanding of Jesus as your personal example in life. This chapter could dramatically change and refresh your approach to a spiritual habit long overlooked.

> **Truth #1**
>
> **Prayer is the True Source of a Believer's Guidance and Power**

If we desire to live a life of faith, then we must walk as Jesus did (see 1 John 2:6). Jesus is the ultimate figure of faith.

The Humanity of Jesus

Before Jesus burst forth with divine glory, he did something very human. He climbed a mountain (God doesn't climb mountains, he's already there) and he prayed. In fact, he was in the act of praying when he was transfigured.

A common question is this: If Jesus was God in the flesh, why did he need to pray? And to whom was he praying? The answer is: God the Son is fully God. He took on human form and limited himself to time and space when he came into our world. Having become like us in our humanity, Jesus knew what it was like to walk by faith. He had to rely on the Holy Spirit to guide, empower, and speak to him.

Jesus Is our Example

We know that Jesus is supposed to be our example in everything. He is our faith leader. But doesn't that seem problematic? Because he's God, and I'm not. My wife told me so. (That I'm not God, that is.) It seems like the math doesn't work. It doesn't seem fair for God to expect me to follow the example of Jesus if Jesus is totally different than me.

Here's something huge, and it will change your life when you fully come to realize this: We do not deeply identify with the life of Jesus as an example for our lives because we think he had no idea what a real problem was.

How could Jesus know what it's like not to be able to pay bills, or get sick. We think Jesus didn't have real problems. He just *miracled* his problems away. We assume we can't do the stuff he did. He may have come to our sandbox, but we think he's a little like Clark Kent. He might be in our world, but he's got powers available to him that are not available to us.

Because we assume Jesus was so different than us, we then inadvertently think his advice and leadership in our lives is not really going to be helpful. How can Jesus help us practically when he lived so far above us?

We couldn't be more wrong.

The truth is—Jesus played by our rules? That changes everything, doesn't it? If we believed Jesus dealt with real problems with the same resources we have, then we would rely on him a lot more. We would trust him, because he's been in similar messes.

So, if Jesus lived by our rules, how did he accomplish so much? How did he do miracles? I don't go around raising dead people, and I'll bet you don't either.

Jim and Carol Cymbala

Jim and Carol Cymbala have an amazing story of faith. They pastor the Brooklyn Tabernacle, and reach many different kinds of people there in New York. In particular, Jim shared that they reach many who are down and out—kids from the street, former drug users. Carol began taking these people, who were truly broken, and put them in the choir. Now, frankly, the choir is amazing! They even sang at Carnegie Hall. One day a man came up to Carol and said, "I don't get it! You take these people off the street, and now they're singing these incredible songs all over the world. How do you do it? What's your secret?

"I'll tell you her secret in a few pages. First, let's look at just how human Jesus was.

The Limitations Jesus put on Himself

In the incarnation, when God became flesh, God limited himself. That means he experienced humanness. Philippians 2:7 tells us that he made himself nothing and took on human likeness. That is, he set aside his rights and privileges

British scholar and medical doctor, Martin Lloyd Jones, wrote:

> [Jesus] deliberately put limits on himself. Now we cannot go further. We do not know how he did it. We cannot understand it, in a sense. But we believe this; in order that he might live this life as a man, while he was here on earth, he did not exercise certain qualities of his Godhead.

By choosing to limit himself, he was able to fully understand being human and the need to exercise faith. So, when we study Jesus in the Gospels, we are seeing perfect faith at work.

Let's look at a few ways that Jesus limited himself, just so you will have confidence that he really was more like you than you may have ever imagined.

Jesus limited his presence. In Heaven, God is omnipresent. He's everywhere! He is at every star, every tree, ever blade of grass. He can be in the center of the earth, to the highest heights. There is nowhere God cannot be. It's impossible for us to identify with that! We might think it sounds like fun to be everywhere at once, but we really can't even fully take the idea in. When Jesus came to earth, he limited his presence. He rode on a donkey, traveled in a boat, and walked from one place to another.

Jesus limited his power. Jesus did miracles because of his relationship with the Father. In fact, in John 14:11 he asked his disciples to believe that he was in the Father and the Father in him. What evidence did he have to prove his relationship with the Father? The evidence of miracles. Jesus was able to do miracles because he had an unbroken connection with God. There was no static (no sin) between him and the Father.

> *I tell you the truth, the Son can do nothing by himself; he can do only what he sees his Father doing, because whatever the Father does the Son also does.*
>
> — John 5:19

His power came from God in Heaven. In Mark 6 he came to his home town, and the text clearly notes that he could do no miracles there because of their disbelief. It would seem as though that Jesus desired to do miracles, but the Father did offer his power because he saw the hearts of the people. Jesus' power did not come from himself, it came from God in Heaven.

Jesus limited his knowledge. God in Heaven knows every little thing that happens. He knows every hair that falls. He knows the sparrow. He even knows when a mountain goat gives birth. God knows every big thing that happens. He knows the stars by name. When Jesus became flesh, for those 33 years on earth, Jesus limited his knowledge.

In the Gospel of John, Jesus emphasized many times that even his teaching was not his own. What was special about his teaching was that it came from the Father (see John 7:16, 8:27-28, 12:49, 14:10, 14:24).

How did Jesus know all those things it seems like no other human knew? The Father told him. His relationship to the Father gave him insights that were incredible.

Jesus limited his decisions. He submitted to the will of the Father. In Heaven, God does not ask for permission to do anything. He is by nature Sovereign. But the Son on earth submitted himself to the Father. In fact, on the night before he died, Jesus asked that the cup be taken from him. But then he asked not that his own will be accomplished, but that God's will from Heaven be done.

Chapter 3—Jesus' Secret

Submission in Jesus' life was a constant decision. When he was arrested, he told those who bound him, *"Do you not think that I cannot appeal to my Father, and he will at once send me more than twelve legions of angels?"* (Matthew 26:53, ESV). But he did not ask the father to send angels. He submitted his will to God's will.

Consider these. Could Jesus fully understand us if he never had to pray for the answer to a problem? If Jesus never submitted to a decision he didn't personally like, would he really know what it was like to obey God in a fallen world? If Jesus just used a miracle for his personal pleasure and comfort, would we really truly feel he could give us an example on how to live? The answer to each is—No!

Jesus became fully human; and he didn't cheat. He did not use power or knowledge that we do not also have available to us.

What Jesus Did That Was Not Limited

Jesus might have limited his presence and knowledge and power and even submitted to the Father, but there is something important he did not limit—his nature. Just because he limited himself does not mean at any time that he ceased to be God.

Jesus did not limit his heart when he came to earth. His love for God and man was huge and infinite. His love far exceeded even our capacity to love. In Jesus we observe the unbridled love of God. Likewise, he did not limit his justice, or his hate for sin, or his concern for the outcast. In Jesus we see the nature of God in full force.

Jesus also did not limit his spiritual authority. He maintained the authority as Son of God to forgive sins. He also displayed supreme authority over Satan. Jesus did not defeat Satan with his power. They did not go into the desert and have a wrestling match to see who was stronger physically. They didn't arm wrestle. Jesus does not defeat Satan simply by his power, but by his person. Satan cannot withstand the person of God. Jesus' essence, his very being, his life, defeats Satan. It's not just that God is bigger than the devil. In Jesus we see that at the core—God is better.

What Was Jesus' Secret

If Jesus played by our rules—if he didn't cheat and use power not available to us—then how did he live such an extraordinary life? It would seem that even God would need to rely on a few tricks to get by in the world, right? But Jesus didn't need a single trick. He never cheated. Not once did he reach into a bag for a tool that we don't also have in our bag.

Notice the people closest to Jesus also lived exceptional lives. Peter, John, and James—the three who had gone with him up the mountain, would be a part of incredible things in the days ahead. Why did they live such exceptional lives? Because they knew the secret. It seems that the further Christianity gets from the life of Jesus, the more we lose sight of the secret.

So, what was his secret? Jesus did not have a prayer time—he had a prayer life.

He stayed in constant, direct contact with God. His every move was directed by God in Heaven. He prayed over every decision. God was able to lead him and give him everything he needed because Jesus never broke contact. As a result, Jesus was an open channel for God to work through.

If you spent time with Jesus, what should amaze you is how much time he spent praying. Prayer was a really big deal to Jesus! He takes three of his friends up a mountain. For what purpose? This is not just a hike—Jesus wanted to go up there to pray.

Some of you are probably already thinking—if I have access to the same resources Jesus did, and Jesus raised dead people and walked on water—does that mean that I can raise dead people and walk on water? Can I do miracles? The answer is—you can do anything God wants you to do. Anything he commands you to do. Probably, God has never wanted you to raise the dead. He's never commanded you to walk on water. But if the need arose, he could quickly and easily empower you. After all, not only did Jesus walk on water—so did Peter.

As long as we maintain an unbroken connection with the Father through prayer, we will be empowered by God to live exactly the life he wants us to. We don't have to live a life exactly like Jesus lived. He lived the life of the Messiah. That was his purpose. We don't have to fill that role. But we do have to live our life in whatever role we are in exactly the way Jesus would fulfill that life. Your question should be—how would Jesus do this? You don't need to be a miracle workin' Messiah. You need to be like Jesus in the role you're in.

Chapter 3—Jesus' Secret

Break New Ground with God

Take a moment to reflect—how would this week be different if you prayed constantly? You would have more peace; you would make better decisions; you'd please the flesh less and the Father more; you'd be more loving and much more purpose driven. In fact, if you prayed more this week, you would have a much higher level of personal focus. If you prayed more this coming week, your words would have more meaning, your faith would be more daring—everything would be radically different.

You might be saying, "Wait a minute! I want to know how to really find newness in my spiritual life. I want to go spiritually where I've never gone before. And your answer is just prayer?" No. My answer is that we must pray differently.

Most believers are familiar with prayer. What is new is the idea that prayer is to be a constant dialogue with God in which we share with him and he in return directs and empowers our path ahead.

Jesus was addicted to prayer the way some people are addicted to their phone. Do you know someone who can't go anywhere or do anything without being near their phone? Their phone is their life. Jesus was that way about prayer. He didn't go anywhere or do anything without prayer. Some people won't make a decision without doing a web search first. Jesus didn't make a move without prayer. For him, prayer wasn't an obligation; it was the vital connection to the Father that he depended on. He wouldn't stop praying. Jesus prayed *for* others; he prayed *with* others; he prayed *alone*; he prayed in *storms*; he prayed when there were *problems*; and he prayed on a *mountain*.

Back to Jim and Carol

Jim and Carol took people from the streets and put them in the great Brooklyn Tabernacle choir. A man one day asked them the secret of their success. What musical secret were they using that so transformed this group? Carol told him, "Before we practice, or go on a trip, or do anything, we pray together."

"That's great, but what's your musical secret?"

She went over it again—we pray together. And when he pressed her further, she finally said, "Listen, that's my secret. Prayer. We pray. Prayer is the power this thing runs on."

Follow the Example of Jesus

When we understand how much Jesus became like us, then his life becomes an example we can follow. His example is only frustrating when we don't understand the source of his knowledge and power. Jesus relied totally on the Father in Heaven. Now, Jesus himself is in Heaven ready to help us. That means that following Jesus' example goes from being impossible to doable.

While Jesus was on earth, God sent the Holy Spirit to guide him. Jesus promised he would not leave us as orphans, but would send us that very same help. Because of what Jesus did for us on the cross, and because the Holy Spirit dwells in us—God's children also have a unique relationship with the Father in Heaven. What does God want us to do? Follow Jesus—stop saying it's impossible—stop complaining that we can't follow him. He wants us to take a deep breath and do what we never thought possible—live like Jesus.

Put Truth #1 into Action

The first truth in breaking new ground with God is confidence in the power of prayer. Not just prayer to get what we want, but prayer as our guide and source of power.

Did your prayer time just get nuked? Did it suddenly blow up? Do you want to open the floodgates of your prayer time? Take a look at Jesus and think—if he needed to pray, then I really need to pray. Hopefully you do nothing without prayer.

The secret to living a life of faith—a life like Jesus—is rooted in constant prayer.

How Can we Pray Constantly?

Are you thinking: I can't pray constantly! I have many things I have to do, I don't have time to always be praying. How can I bow my head, close my eyes and pray all the time?

Prayer is a spiritual exercise, not just a physical posture. Surely, you already knew that. Your spirit can be in constant prayer even as you go through the activities of the day. Prayer is talking to God and listening to him. Paul commanded us to:

> [P]ray in the Spirit on all occasions with all kinds of prayers and requests. With this in mind, be alert and always keep on praying for all the saints.
>
> — Ephesians 6:18

Chapter 3—Jesus' Secret

It is the Holy Spirit we pray to because he lives in us. He is well aware of our thoughts. And Paul suggests our prayers to him are to be non-stop. Note the words, *on all occasions* and *always keep on praying*.

Have you ever heard someone say, "Prayer wears me out?" What's going on? They're doing a lot of asking. And believe it or not, asking gets tiring. We think of someone who needs prayer, and we start asking for stuff.

"Lord, I pray for Judy. You know she's in the hospital. Please heal her." Then we think of stuff for God to do, so we add, "and God, make her hospital bed comfortable." That wasn't good, God needs more to work with, so we add, "and Lord, I pray even the food taste good. And that she is up and well soon."

We start getting tired as our creativity is tested.

It's fine, even right, to ask for things from God. It's good to be specific. But if that is the only way we pray, then we are missing a lot.

Prayer is also fellowship. It's not just asking of God, it's talking to God. It's directing my thoughts to God. In the flesh, we direct our thoughts to ourselves. We talk in our heads to ourselves all the time. Constant prayer requires retraining ourselves to remember that the Holy Spirit dwells in our inner-most being, and that he is listening to our thoughts.

"Hey now, wait a minute!" you may be thinking, "I don't know how to direct thoughts to God. I don't even know if I want God listening in on my thoughts."

Once you start to direct your thoughts toward God, and you force yourself to do it for a period of time, soon it begins to come natural to you. Like riding a bike. This inner prayer time does not replace our need for structured prayer time. Times when we expend greater energy going through needs and lifting things and people up to God. But it does move us to a place of constant communication with God. And sometimes, as you think through an issue, God will interrupt you and ask you to give more attention in prayer to something.

"Pause and put that to words," the Spirit might direct, "Pray that one through more seriously."

I told a man in our community I would pray for him. Each time I drove by his shop, I thought kindly about him. One day as I drove by, the Holy Spirit interrupted me "David, I don't just want you to think good thoughts about him. I want you to pray with words for that man."

It's hard to offer God all your thoughts, and think nasty things about your spouse. You cannot be in constant communication with God and be planning to do something immoral or unethical. You cannot be constantly praying and at the same time lusting after one of God's children.

Constant communion with God makes our thought life an offering to God. And we allow God to interrupt our thoughts with his correction, insights, or direction.

A Breakthrough Prayer

Just asking for more stuff wears us down quickly. But there is a simple prayer that can be transformational to our walk. It is a prayer we can pray in any situation. It's this, "God, show me." Show me—*what you're doing here.* Show me—*what's really going on.* Show me—*how to respond.*

Our eyes are easily blinded to spiritual realities that God sees. Elisha's servant couldn't see the chariots of fire surrounding his enemies until Elisha prayed for his servant's eyes to be opened. God is doing things all around us, but we easily focus only on what we can see naturally. We trust our eyes, our emotions, and our instincts to tell us what is really going on. But all three of those things can lead us to terrible responses.

Next time you're in a difficult conversation, silently ask God to show you what he's doing in the other persons life. He might show you pain, you overlooked. Or he might remind you of something they shared with you long ago that you had forgotten all about. The Holy Spirit inside you can direct you in amazing ways if you constantly communicate to him you are willing to be used. Throughout the day, just ask God over and over, "Show me." Ask him in your work place, "God, *show me* why my coworker is so upset today. *Show me* how to minister to my coworker." Ask him in your home, "Lord, would you *show me* the best way to discipline this child? Why is this child hurting so deeply? Would you *show me* what's really going on?" Ask him as you talk to a grieving friend, "Lord, *show me* how to love this person and not just say something trite."

When you ask God to show you what he is doing, you are asking to be on his team. You are submitting to his will. The "Show me" prayer can be a constant connection point between you and God.

An Encouraging Note

Do you ever feel like God takes way too long to answer a prayer request? We all do! God never moves at our pace.

In Deuteronomy 3:23, Moses reveals a prayer request he took to the Lord. He didn't ask that his congregation treat him better, or pay him more, or that he get into a good college. Moses asked God to allow him to go into the Promised Land. He'd heard so much about it! He'd heard the report from the spies of a land flowing with milk and honey.

The text doesn't just say that Moses asked God if he could enter the Promised Land—it says he *pleaded* with God. But God told Moses to stop asking.

Moses died on Mount Nebo looking down into the Promised Land. God buried him and Jude tells us that the Devil and the angel Michael fought over the body of Moses. It would seem there is no way God was going to answer Moses' prayer request.

Then there was the day that Jesus went up mountain to pray. And who should appear with Jesus but Moses and Elijah. If Jesus did indeed transfigure at the traditional site of Mount Tabor they were well within the boundaries of the Promised Land. Moses not only saw the land of Israel from Heaven, God allowed him for a moment to step down onto the earth and stand in the very land he'd begged God to enter about 1400 years earlier.

I imagine there must have been a day in Heaven when God called, "Hey, Moses, come here!"

Moses scrambled to God's side, "Me? Now?"

"Didn't you ask to go across the Jordan? Didn't you want to go into the Promised Land?"

"Yes, Lord. But that was a long time ago. And I've already seen it from here."

"Well, I'm going to let you more than just look at it. I'm going to take you and Elijah down there with me."

God can answer our prayers in ways we never imagined. It may take him years. He may answer some after we're dead. Just because something is taking a long time, doesn't mean God's done. Now he may tell you, like he did Moses, to stop praying about it—he's heard your prayer and he'll make a decision. Or, he may ask you to keep on praying over an issue for years.

People of faith must be people of prayer. It is our source of direction from God. And it allows us to present problems and requests to God—trusting his answer.

What God is Doing with Answered Prayer

In the Bible God has given us his résumé. He has shown us his credentials to handle any problem we have. Though he doesn't have to prove himself to us, he has shown us that he is absolutely capable of running this world! Not only does God show us his power in the Bible, but it becomes very personal through answered prayer.

When God Answers Prayer...

1. **He is training our heart to trust him.** When he asks us to do something we can simply obey with faith. We don't have to worry about the details or even the end result—we just have to obey. In fact, he may not show us the end result until we take the first steps of obedience. It's the not knowing that makes it faith!

2. **He is training us to know that he will take care of us.** We all love the Charlie Brown cartoons. Every time Charlie Brown is going to kick the football, Lucy is there holding the ball for him. What does she do? Every time—every single time—as Charlie runs at the football, at just the last second, Lucy would pull the ball up. Ole Charlie Brown is always seen flipping and flying in circles as his feet shoot up in the air. Would you trust Lucy to take care of you? No way! She doesn't have a proven track record. But God does. Every time he answers prayer, he's telling you that he will provide for you.

3. **He is challenging us to pray bigger.** *"If you remain in me and my words remain in you, ask whatever you wish, and it will be given you. This is to my Father's glory, that you bear much fruit, showing yourselves to be my disciples"* (John 15:7-8). The requirement is that we *remain* (Greek: *meno*) in him. If we are faithful to *his* work and *his* Word, then he assures us that anything we ask for will be done for us. Why do our prayers keep getting bigger? Because the problems keep getting bigger. The more you follow Jesus, the bigger the mountains will be.

Chapter 3—Jesus' Secret

Digging Deeper

1. Is it difficult to see Jesus as your example for daily living?

   [ ] Yes   [ ] No   [ ] Sometimes

   Why?
   _____
   _____

2. Constant prayer requires more than just asking God for stuff.

   - Have you ever planned your prayers ahead of time?

     [ ] Never   [ ] Sometimes   [ ] Often   [ ] Always

   - What are some things you can constantly thank God for?
     _____
     _____

   - What are some things you can praise God for?
     _____
     _____

   - What prayer did God recently answer?
     _____

   - Who is someone you are especially thankful for?
     _____

   - What has God done recently that fills you with joy?
     _____
     _____
     _____

Break New Ground With God

3. What time of the day have you devoted as your prayer time? This is a time we structure for asking, praising and giving thanks.

_____

_____

_____

_____

4. Jesus chose to pray with three of his apostles. Who is someone you would like to spend more time praying with?

_____

_____

_____

_____

5. What are you praying for now that you prayed for 2 years ago?

_____

_____

_____

_____

6. What would change if you directed all your thoughts to God?

_____

_____

_____

_____

4 Put The Awe Back In Awesome

Who among the gods is like you, O LORD? Who is like you—majestic in holiness, awesome in glory, working wonders?
Exodus 15:11

Our culture uses *awesome* pretty flippantly. "Awesome dude, far out!" "You gotta try those hotdogs, they're awesome!" Or, how about, "His house is wicked awesome."

> **Truth #2**
>
> **A personal sense of awe and wonder is vital to our spiritual health**

Some of those statements are just jamming words together. They do not in any way reflect the true meaning of awesome.

Rich Mullens wrote the inspiring song *Awesome God*. Nothing else fully encompasses the meaning of awesome more than the Almighty God. After crossing the Red Sea, Moses declared:

> *Who is like you—*
> *majestic in holiness,*
> *awesome in glory,*
> *working wonders?*
>
> — Exodus 15:11

On the Mount of Transfiguration the disciples encountered the *Awesome God*. Their response was completely appropriate; they fell on their faces in holy fear. They were terrified! Don't judge them, because you would have been, too. This is not just an earthly response. In Revelation, we are shown the courts of Heaven, and even the Heavenly beings fall down before the Almighty. The apostles are very aware that they have been very close to God.

An element we may be too quick to brush off as just emotionalism is the importance of AWE in our walk with God. Rational faith, we figure, does not need to get caught up in emotionalism.

My soul needs something (someone) bigger than me to stand in awe of. Awe of God is vital to our spiritual health. Awe is more than just the acknowledgement that God is big, sovereign, mighty, or even eternal. It is a welling up in our hearts that says, "Wow! I have been in the presence of something wonderful and scary and big, and my heart is stirred!"

My heart longs for someone not just like me, but someone bigger than me. I have a need in my life to worship. In fact, left on my own, I will worship the wrong things. I will worship money, sex, sports, food, doughnuts, steak, jelly beans—sorry, I got stuck on food.

The reformer, John Calvin, memorably said that the heart is an idol factory. That is, we will worship something or someone. If we don't find what is true and worship there, then we will build something false and worship that. But we will worship. Even if we have to mold it, build it, or feed it—we will worship something. At the Transfiguration, God directed our attention to his Son, Jesus.

Hopefully, this chapter will nudge you toward awe. To encourage you to think deeply about the person of Christ and to worship him in your heart. To give yourself permission to say in your heart, or out loud, "Wow! I serve an awesome God!"

The Disciples Response

The disciples did not know how to respond to Jesus' Transfiguration. They were probably excited, wowed, full of awe—and then terrified as the cloud passed over them and the voice from Heaven spoke.

It might surprise you to know that fear is a vital component to experiencing awe. Matthew 17:6 says that when the disciples heard the voice of God, they fell to the ground on their faces afraid. The Greek, *phobeo*, carries the idea of *being terrified*. The next thing they knew, Jesus is touching them and urging them to get up and *don't be afraid*. Why are they afraid? Because they have just been in the awesome presence of the Almighty.

In Judges 13, Samson's father and mother have a visit from the angel of Yahweh. They think they are simply speaking with a messenger at a fire. Imagine their amazement when suddenly their visitor ascends into Heaven through the fire. Like the disciples on the

Mount of Transfiguration, the couple falls with their faces to the ground. They did not have Jesus to put a comforting hand on their shoulder and tell them not to be afraid. Terrified, the man says to his wife, "*We are doomed to die! We have seen God!*" But his wife is not so sure. "*I think if God meant to kill us, I don't think he would have accepted our offering or promised us a child.*"

Glory, fear, and awe all seem to be themes that bump into one another. None of them are the same. The progression often happens like this: first humans somehow encounter the glory of God; then there is fear mixed with awe; then awareness on the part of mortal man that he has stood in the presence of the Almighty.

God Shows us Jesus' Glory

The Gospels tell us that Jesus' body underwent a transformation. Luke 9:32 says that at the Transfiguration, when the apostles *became fully awake*, they saw the *glory* of Jesus. They also saw Jesus' two visitors. Now Jesus' normal state of being while he was on earth, incarnate, was not light. He didn't have a halo. So, why on this occasion was Jesus radiating with light?

One preacher suggested that at the Transfiguration, we actually see Jesus' full humanity. That is, we see in Jesus sinless humanity. Perhaps even Adam and Eve once glowed in their sinless state. But the fall marred creation, and thus mankind no longer glows. But in Jesus, at the Transfiguration, his true full unhindered humanity bursts forth and we see what we will be one day.

While that's interesting, there seems to be a pretty basic problem. Nowhere are humans described as *light*. But the very being of God is described as *light* (see 1 John 1:5). What burst forth from Jesus at the Transfiguration was not his human nature, but his divine glory.

The word order is worth observing here. Matthew 17:2 literally reads, "*And he was transfigured before them and shone the face of him as the sun—and the clothes of him became white as the light.*" First his face glowed, then his clothes. Unlike Moses, who glowed from an external source (he had been in the presence of God's glory on Mount Sinai) Jesus glowed from an internal source—God's glory was within him coming out. He wasn't shined on, he shined out.

Why did Jesus radiate with light? This was glory coming from him. Glory is often pictured as light. Scholar Herbert Lockyer pointed out, "The word shining or glistening is used of a gleam from polished surfaces, arms, sleek horses, water in motion, the twinkling of stars, lightening." In fact, like a flash of lightning is how the Gospel of Luke describes Jesus' appearance.

God was showing the disciples the glory of Jesus. Before Jesus came to earth, while he was in Heaven, he shined with physical glory.

John was present at the Transfiguration and made mention of it in his gospel—albeit in a very different way.

> *The Word became flesh and made his dwelling among us. We have seen his glory, the glory of the One and Only, who came from the Father, full of grace and truth.*
>
> — John 1:14

The words, *made his dwelling among us* could also be translated *tabernacled with us*. A tabernacle is a temporary tent. As if Jesus' earthly body was but a tent within which hid the Shekinah glory. Then, in the same verse, John declares that he and others have seen Jesus' glory. When did John see Jesus' glory if it was hidden inside the tabernacle of his body? At the Transfiguration.

In 2005 scientist in the everglades discover a python that had exploded. What happened? A python usually eats animals such as antelope, monkeys, rodents, lizards, birds, and caimans (small alligator-like animals). But this python ate an alligator. The result wasn't pretty. The Transfiguration is like a spiritual explosion. The glory of God bursts forth in radiant light, causing even his cloths to transform. While the results of a python eating an alligator aren't pretty, the result of God's glory beaming from Jesus is all together beautiful. For a moment on the mountain, the disciples saw with their eyes what they had been experiencing every day of their journey with Jesus. If love, compassion, joy, and the inner being of God could be physically manifested, it was that day in the physical glory of Jesus.

Isaiah saw Jesus' Glory

In John 12 there is an extended conversation about the glory of Jesus. As he considers his coming death, what he calls his *hour*, Jesus says that he has made a decision not to ask the father to save him from this hour. Instead he prayed that God will glorify his name in his suffering. That is, the death of Jesus would bring glory to God the Father. In response to Jesus' prayer, God speaks from Heaven and declares that he has glorified it (in Jesus' life), and will glorify it again, this time in Jesus' death.

Considering the idea that Jesus was going to die, someone asked a good question. Shouldn't the Christ remain forever? So, how could Jesus say he was going to die? John explains that they did not understand and did not believe him because their hearts were hard. And then John says something amazing.

> Isaiah said this because he saw Jesus' glory and spoke about him.
>
> — John 12:41

As a prophet, Isaiah had seen Jesus in Heaven and had specifically observed Jesus' glory.

So, before Jesus came into the world, he illuminated with glory. When Jesus came to earth, he limited himself to a human body and set aside his glory. But at the Transfiguration, his glory once again burst forth. Glory that Isaiah had seen.

When exactly did Isaiah see Jesus' glory? In Isaiah 6, God swept Isaiah into the courts of Heaven where he saw the throne of Heaven, and on the throne highly exalted was the Lord. Amazing six-winged seraphs ascended and descended on him, declaring to one another the holiness and might of God. They declare that the earth is *full of his glory*. As they sing and shout God's might, the dwelling of God shakes and fills with smoke. It's an amazing moment. Isaiah realizes he is seriously messed up. "*I'm ruined!*" he cries. But God not only makes him holy, but sends him on a mission to go and preach. And there in Heaven, he hears God tell him the spiritual condition of the people of Israel (see Isaiah 6:9-10). Obviously, this is the same event where Isaiah saw Jesus' glory.

This is exciting because it means that Isaiah did not only see God the Father, but saw the glory of God the Son as well. Jesus' glory is not just something that would come in the future, it is something Jesus possessed for all eternity. Glory is part of his eternal being.

Jesus Ascended to Glory

Not only was Jesus glory something that shined in the past, but after the ascension the apostles gave testimony in Acts 3:13 that God had *glorified* Jesus. The physical attributes of his glory were restored to him. Remember, Paul was temporarily blinded when he encountered the risen, glorified Jesus on the Damascus road.

The Apostle John, who was with Jesus on the Mount of Transfiguration, says in Revelation 1 that he was imprisoned on the Island of Patmos. On the island, he had a very powerful encounter with the glorified Jesus. John reports that Jesus' hair was white *like wool* or as *white as snow*. He describes Jesus' voice as rushing water—full of power and might. In describing Jesus' face, John writes:

> *His face was like the sun shining in all its brilliance.*
>
> — Revelation 1:16

Imagine John's excitement. He who stood on the mountain and saw Jesus' Transfiguration—who reported that he had personally seen the glory of the One and Only—encounters the glorified Christ once again in what must have been his own darkest hour. As the church on earth suffered and the apostle grew old on a prison island, how amazing it was for him to see the savior's glory. The darkness of the world did not for one moment decrease God's power.

Glory is More Than Light

Why is glory important? Because it is a quality of God. For Jesus to have glory is evidence of his divine nature. He is not just another person we want to hang out with—Jesus is God. That means that he has all the attributes of God, all the authority of God, the full character of God. He does not simply show us God—he *is* God.

Glory is God's character—holiness, beauty, perfection—his exaltation above all things. His physical glory is an outward manifestation of his virtues.

John Piper compared God's glory to his holiness. Piper said, God's glory "is the way he puts his holiness on display for people to apprehend. So, the glory of God is the holiness of God made manifest."

One way we see God's holiness is through shiny light. But God's glory is more than light. God's glory expresses the heart of who he is. So, when Jesus came to earth, while he did not normally glow with God's glory, his character and person still displayed the glory of God. In the Gospels, as Jesus interacts with people, heals the sick, talks to the despised—we are witnessing the glory of God. We witness the glory of God in the Gospels as Jesus interacts with people, heals the sick and talks to the despised. When Jesus submitted to the Father and went to the cross, he was showing us the glory of God.

Chapter 4—Put The Awe Back In Awesome

Even the miracles of Jesus are a display of God's glory—a demonstration that the Creator stands above the physical limitations of the creation. Luke 5 describes an interesting account where Jesus was teaching from a boat. When he finished speaking, he told Peter to steer the boat into the deep water and let down the next.

Peter was exhausted, they had already been up all night and caught nothing. However, because Jesus directed him to, Peter sailed the boat back into the deep water and let down his net. As soon as they were let down, the nets were swamped with fish. They caught such a large number of fish their nets began to break and the boats began to sink. Overwhelmed, Peter fell on his knees before Jesus. "*Away from me, Lord,*" he cried, "*I am a sinful man.*"

Peter was having an Isaiah moment. Only, one happened on earth, the other happened in Heaven. When Isaiah saw the glory of God, he was convicted of his own sinfulness and said:

> *Woe to me! ... I am ruined! For I am a man of unclean lips, and I live among a people of unclean lips, and my eyes have seen the King, the Lord Almighty.*
>
> — Isaiah 6:5

Peter had a very similar response. Not because he encountered shiny light or singing angels, but because he suddenly realized he was in the presence of God. That is, it's not just the physical attribute of light that causes us to stand in awe of God; the very person of God will drive us to our knees.

The first thing both Peter and Isaiah realized was that they were sinful and unclean. They did not deserve to stand in the presence of such perfection.

Jesus came to show us God. Even the glory of God. Yet, if he did not usually march around glowing—what of God and of God's glory did he intend to show us? The glory of his compassion. The glory of his mercy, kindness, goodness, and love. We see God's character in Jesus. We understand God best through Jesus. That is partly because Jesus came so close to us. He came down into our world in a visible tangible way. It is also because he set aside the physical attribute of his glory—light—and showed us instead the deeper part of his glory. It is like God had to dim the light of his physical glory when Jesus came into the world so that we might see his spiritual glory. But at the Transfiguration, the lights were on full blast! Maybe. Or maybe even the disciples did not see the glory full blast. Could earthly eyes bear such a sight?

In his wonderful book on *Systematic Theology*, Dr. Wayne Grudem writes about the glory of God, saying that the glory of God:

> is the visible manifestation of the excellence of God's character. The greatness of God's being, the perfection of all his attributes, is something that we can never fully comprehend, but before which we can only stand in awe and worship. (p. 221)

Notice glory and awe go together. God shines his glory, his character, his excellence—and we mortals stand in awe. Awe is a wonderful emotion that leaves you feeling small and breathless and excited and even fearful in the presence of One much more mighty than us.

How is the creation to feel in the presence of the Creator? Amazed. Humbled. Afraid. Awestruck. And we need those things. In fact, our souls crave the bigness of God.

Mark Altrogge is a pastor and songwriter. He often puts Scripture to music. He's written, *I'm Forever Grateful* (2004), *You are Beautiful* (2004), and the classic, *I Stand in Awe* (1999).

Mark says that during the time that he wrote *I Stand in Awe*, he was reading several books about God—his holiness and attributes. Mark was overcome with the fact that God is infinite. He wrote in an April 2015 article for the *Blazing Center*:

> I was particularly blown away to learn that God is an infinite being, and infinite in each of his attributes. He is infinitely holy. Infinitely powerful. Infinitely loving. Infinitely wise. In fact, because he is infinite, there will always be things about himself that only He knows. Throughout eternity, those he redeemed will never come to an end of seeing new vistas of his glory, majesty and beauty.

Putting Truth into Action

Awe is an emotional, intellectual, worshipful response to the power, might and holiness of God. Awe is a response to God's glory.

Awe is an emotional response. When we stand in awe of God, our hearts soar. We are filled with a mixture of fear and joy—that mixture can be described as awe. It is breathtaking. Our very soul can quake in fear, and yet excitement and joy pounds through us at the same time. It's what John felt when he fell at Jesus' feet on the Island of Patmos. It's what Peter felt when he knelt down in the fishing boat. It's what Isaiah felt when he stood in the courts of Heaven

Chapter 4—Put The Awe Back In Awesome

and saw the Almighty. It's what Thomas felt when he pressed his hand into Jesus' and declared, "*My Lord and my God.*"

We so crave that in our culture, we become thrill seekers. We want something that will make our heart pound with amazement at something bigger than us. So, we thunder down roller coasters and ride waves on surfboards. All fun stuff, but nothing compares to the awe of encountering the mighty God.

God is worthy of my awe. In an episode of *Modern Marvels* the modern marvel they were focused on was ... drum roll ... the *can opener*. I thought, "Modern Marvels has run out of the Marvelous!" We think we're advanced because we can preserve food, open cans, and launch a man into space. In perspective, we serve one who stretched the universe.

Awe is a worshipful response. Beyond just an emotional thrill, awe causes our very soul to skip a beat and say, "Oh God, you are Amazing!" Like Peter, it drives us to our knees wherever we are. Have you ever stood on a hill top on a starry night and looked up? As you stared at the stars, did you stand in awe of the one who made them? Ever been in awe of God as you looked at a sunset? I've been in awe of God at a church invitation, as people poured down the aisle to kneel down in response to God's message. I've been in awe of God as my children were born, taking their first breaths, joy filled my heart and I was very aware that someone much bigger than me or my wife had created and given them life.

A heart stirred to awe is a heart that breathlessly realizes, "I need this! I want this! I'm scared of this!" all at once. It causes you to say, "I serve a wonderful God!"

Awe is an intellectual response. I saved this for last because we don't often equate awe as something that happens to the mind. Awe allows the mind to rise to new heights. A scientist can discover something new, and stand in awe at that moment of the one who created it. Each of us can stand in awe of God when we learn something we had not previously known about God. When you are studying God's Word, and you make a new discovery, you feel excited, even breathless. That intellectual awe is your mind reaching toward God.

The Bible commands us to worship God with our mind. Intellectual awe, worshiping God with our mind, is seeking to learn more about God. It is wanting to know his truth, and as you discover it, you are more and more in awe of him.

Break New Ground With God

Remember shortly before the Transfiguration—when Peter declared that Jesus is the Christ, the son of the Living God—Jesus blessed him and said:

[T]his was not revealed to you by man, but by my Father in Heaven.

— Matthew 16:17

God can put thoughts in our minds that cause us to marvel.

Psalm 145:3-5 captures our sense of awe as something that is both too big to be grasped, and yet something that should be thought about over and over:

Great is the LORD and most worthy of praise;
his greatness no one can fathom.

One generation will commend your works to another;
they will tell of your mighty acts.

They will speak of the glorious splendor of your majesty,
and I will meditate on your wonderful works.

— Psalm 145:3-5

The Psalmist writes that God's greatness *no one can fathom*—he is beyond our mind. And yet, he still dares to *meditate* on what he can grasp of God.

Our mind, our heart, and our soul needs to be shaken at the bigness, the power, the infinitude of God. We need to sense his glory. Awe is not only inspirational, it's motivational. Those moments we stand in total amazement of who God is and the reality of his very being, we are moved to press forward in our faith. We suddenly want to learn more, worship more, experience more.

How can I Experience More Awe in my Walk with God?

Psalm 33 tells us:

Let all the earth fear Yahweh;
Let all the inhabitants of the world stand in awe of Him.

— Psalm 33:8

It's not just a national call to stand in awe of God, it is a worldwide demand. Whoever we are, whatever race we are, whatever family we come from or what our occupation is—everyone is to stand in awe of the Almighty.

Notice that Psalm 33:8 is a command: *Let all the inhabitants of the world stand in awe of Him.*

That suggests that awe is as much a choice as it is just an emotional response. We can create the right conditions for us to encounter God in fresh, new ways. We can shepherd our own hearts the right direction. And, in the right moment, wonder and amazement are even emotional choices we can make.

1. Worship in community. Every worship service is not going to lift you to new heights. But more often than not, as I stand with my local church in worship, I feel truly in awe of God. As I worship God, my own heart is moved and prepared to experience his presence. In particular, both singing and preaching stir my intellect and my emotions.

2. Root out sin. Sin chokes our walk with God. It is spiritually devastating. I don't think anyone would want to claim to be more righteous than the prophet Isaiah. Yet, when Isaiah stood in the presence of God, even he was convicted of his sinful condition.

It is worth noting that the particular sin Isaiah was grieved over was his mouth.

> *'Woe to me!' I cried. 'I am ruined! For I am a man of unclean lips, and I live among a people of unclean lips, and my eyes have seen the King, the LORD Almighty.'*
>
> — Isaiah 6:5

A young man and his wife began attending our church. They got into a home group and advocated drug use as a means of experiencing God more dynamically. We quickly removed them from our home group ministry. However, one night the young man showed up at a praise team practice. I asked him what he was doing at the church, as he clearly desired to teach our congregation things I believed were heretical.

This young man, a United States Marine, began to brag to me about his spiritual walk with God. "God lifted me to the ****** Heavens." But where I have stars, he cursed. And then he said, "I saw God. I was **** blown away." And he went on and on.

Finally, I said, "I do not believe you saw God. I don't believe any of your story."

Shaken he asked why I did not believe him.

Break New Ground With God

"Because when Isaiah saw the Lord, he was specifically convicted about his mouth. And not just his mouth, but his entire community's mouth. I think if you truly saw God, your first response would not be to brag to me, your first response would be to say, 'woe is me, I am ruined! This is going to destroy me!' And you would begin to take sin very serious."

Our sin can hold back our joy in Christ. It robs us of our awe and ties us down to the gritty, dirty confines of this world. But when we choose to give up sinful behaviors, we are set free to stand in awe of God. Our hearts are allowed to soar once again. Worship becomes joyful when we break free from sin and our minds are not polluted with a sense of guilt but are unchained to think about God.

3. Take time in nature. Some of the greatest moments I have had worshiping God have come as I climbed up steep hills in the desert—the night sky glowing above me and wind blowing in my face. The vastness of the sky is simply amazing. It catches my breath away.

Every aspect of creation can move us to simply be in awe of God. You can be in a forest, near a waterfall, at the ocean, or even in the desert and be overcome with the majesty and creativity of God.

Psalm 8:3-4 is beautiful.

When I consider your Heavens, the work of your fingers,
  the moon and the stars, which you have set in place,
what is man that you are mindful of him,
  the son of man that you care for him?

— Psalm 8:3-4

The Psalmist says, "*When I look at how vast it all is, how big it is, how amazing it is—I am all the more amazed that you care about little us. And yet, you do!*" In that moment, he is not only in awe of the bigness of creation, but the simple truth that God, who is even bigger than all that we can see, loves us so deeply.

4. Listen to stories of faith. Have you ever listened to someone tell about an experience they had with God, and it stirs your own heart to new heights? I love hearing people of faith tell how God has moved them.

Psalm 145 contains the line:

One generation will commend your works to another;
  they will tell of your mighty acts.

— Psalm 145:4

That's not just talking about *Bible days*. Even today, one generation commends God's works to the next generation. From testimonies in church to wonderful accounts of faith your friends share with you.

One reason to get close to some old people of faith is so that you can learn their stories and marvel with them at how God came through in times of crisis. As they share what God did in their life, your faith will grow and you will stand in awe of God with them.

5. Slowdown in God's Word. It is a huge step forward in a persons walk when they decide to read the Bible regularly. At some point in our Christian culture, we have been told that we ought to read the Bible in a year. This leaves many new believers reading as fast as they can, and quite a few giving up mid-year feeling discouraged and defeated. This is not because they failed God, but because they put an arbitrary rule on themselves. We can be so consumed with trying to read large portions of Scripture that we fail to enjoy the Bible.

The Bible is often described like food. It's like bread, or honey, or manna. Sometimes we just need to *slow down and chew*. There are some passages that are so wonderful, they are not meant to be read at eighty miles an hour. As you plow through Psalm 8:3-4, quoted previously, did you speed read through it? In fact, don't rush through any of the Psalms. Hopefully you are not reading them too fast, else, the Holy Spirit will come upon you like the Highway Patrol and pull you over—SLOW DOWN!

Spend time in the Psalms! Even as you read other parts of the Bible, come back again and again to the book of Psalms. It is a worship book full of hymns, praises, poetry, and declarations of the glory of God. As the Psalmist worships, often our own hearts are lifted up with him. As the Psalmist grieves, he teaches our heart how to grieve. When he is angry and prays out his anger, the Psalmist is teaching us how to pray out our anger. In Psalms 150 we encounter God emotionally in a way that is wholly unique to that book.

Digging Deeper

1. Have you previously considered awe to be an important aspect of your walk with God?

    [ ] Yes   [ ] No   [ ] Sometimes

2. What is the most outstanding thing God has done that caused you to stand in awe of him?

    _____
    _____
    _____

3. What are some things that cause you to lose your awe for God?

    _____
    _____

4. The Bible records some incredible moments. Do you have a story (or several) that stirs your faith?

    _____
    _____
    _____

5. In the Gospel of John, Jesus prayed that we be allowed to see his glory.

    Have you ever thought about seeing the glory of Jesus?

    [ ] Yes   [ ] No

    Do you look forward to it?

    _____
    _____
    _____

Chapter 4—Put The Awe Back In Awesome

6. Which of these things most easily stirs awe for God in your heart?
   - [ ] Dynamic worship with other believers.
   - [ ] Being in nature. Things like waterfalls and starry nights.
   - [ ] Reading the Bible.
   - [ ] Moments in prayer when you feel God's presence.
   - [ ] Singing worship songs.
   - [ ] Listening to others tell of miracles and great encounters with God.

7. What do you really worship?

   _____

   _____

   _____

   _____

5 Transforming Power Of The Second Coming

> *We were eyewitnesses of his majesty. For he received honor and glory from God the Father when the voice came to him from the Majestic Glory, saying, 'This is my Son, whom I love; with him I am well pleased.' We ourselves heard this voice that came from heaven when we were with him on the sacred mountain.*
> 2 Peter 2:16-18

Do you ever wish you could go back in time and relive a portion of life knowing then what you know now? In fact, if you could know the future, your entire life would be defined by what's to come.

Truth #3

The Second Coming is a real event that we live toward

In the three synoptic Gospels, Jesus discusses his Second Coming and then says that some who were there with him would not die before they saw it (see Matthew 16:28, Mark 9:1, Luke 9:27). That is a very confusing statement since it's been more than two thousand years, and every one of those who were with Jesus have now died.

Disappointed with Jesus

In Matthew 16, Jesus asked his disciples who people said he was. What was the word on the street? Were people talking about him? Oh, indeed they were! Like today, people had a lot of crazy opinions about who Jesus was. Some thought maybe Jesus was John the Baptist come back from the dead. Of course, that makes no sense, because John baptized Jesus. Others thought Jesus might be the great

Break New Ground With God

prophet Elijah or Jeremiah. Then Jesus got personal. *"What about you? Who do you say I am?"* At that, Peter gave one clear response. *"You are the Christ, the son of the living God."*

There's a *Twilight Zone* episode titled, *A Kind of Stopwatch*. In it, a man receives a stopwatch that can pause time. Of course, he uses this amazing watch to pull all kinds of tricks on those around him. When Peter opens his mouth to answer Jesus' question, it's as if God clicked the stopwatch, paused time and put the words in Peter's mouth.

Peter's response showed confidence in a sea of confusion. Where had he gotten such wisdom? Jesus declared that Peter's words were not his own, he'd spoken under the inspiration of the Father from Heaven. I don't know if this was the first time this had happened to Peter, but it certainly would not be the last. God would often use Peter as his spokesman and even one of the writers of Scripture. Jesus even said that Simon's new name was going to be Peter—*rock*. And on that *rock*—Peter's confession—Jesus was going to establish the bedrock of his movement. Everything would be centered on that one foundational truth: Jesus is the Messiah, the son of God.

Peter must have been swelling with pride. The disciples were excited. Jesus was God's Son, and a huge uprising of some kind was underway, and they were at the center of it. So, what Jesus said next must have caught them totally off guard. He revealed to his disciples exactly what kind of a mission they were on. Jesus said that he would go to Jerusalem and suffer.

Suffer? They expected him to go to Jerusalem and rule. To overturn the religious system, overthrow Rome and toss out the wicked Herods. They did not anticipate him suffering.

More than suffering, Jesus said that he would be killed. By the time he said killed, they were probably so stunned they didn't even hear him say that he would be raised to life on the third day.

How could Jesus take a conversation about his being the Messiah, ready to establish God's Kingdom, and turn it into a proclamation that he was going to die? That was unbelievable to the disciples. Someone needed to speak up and correct Jesus.

Awkward as it was, Peter in his new leadership role felt it must fall on him to try and correct their confused leader. Did Jesus not understand that suffering was not in the game—glory was. In Peter's view, Jesus must have been making a massive leadership mistake.

He'd taken them from seeing the Kingdom of God almost realized, to thoughts of his death. Jesus was only 33, he didn't need to be talking about death. Besides, if he died, then the movement would be over. He was predicting defeat before they even really started.

So, gathering his confidence, Peter pulled Jesus aside and strongly rebuked him. In fact, the Greek word is *epitimao*, to *censure* or *admonish*. It has the idea of forbidding. In our culture, we would say, "No way is this going to happen. Over my dead body!" In Peter's view, and probably the other disciples, Jesus needed to be more positive. He needed to focus on the mission of being Messiah—whatever that involved.

Jesus' response was just as strong as Peter's rebuke. He rebuked Peter's rebuke. *"Get behind me, Satan. You are an offense to me."* In fact, Jesus said, Peter was no longer thinking under the inspiration of Heaven, he was now thinking like a mere man. He wanted to run the ministry in a very worldly way.

Take up your Cross

And then Jesus drops a bomb. Not only is he going to die, but those who follow him must be ready to take up a cross and follow him. If you love your life, you'll lose it, Jesus explains.

The King James Version of the Bible records Jesus' next shocking statement this way:

> *For what is a man profited, if he shall gain the whole world, and lose his own soul? Or what shall a man give in exchange for his soul? For the Son of man shall come in the glory of his Father with his angels; and then he shall reward every man according to his works.*
>
> — Matthew 16:26-28, KJV

The disciples are ready to follow Jesus because they think it means their glory. He wants them to understand up front, that following him means taking up a *cross*. That doesn't mean that everyone who follows Jesus is going to be crucified, but many of those who heard Jesus say this were. To take up your cross and follow Jesus means to give up all of yourself, to die to self, and follow Jesus with supreme devotion. Jesus is telling anyone who wants to be his disciple that they must be totally devoted. Following Jesus is not about saying one quick prayer and assuming you can move on with your life

Break New Ground With God

as you please. Not at all. It means you now submit to Jesus even when it is painful.

The world will make following Jesus very painful. They will accuse followers of being narrow minded and even bigoted for believing God's Word. Those who choose to follow Jesus instead of the culture will lose much. Some will claim to follow Jesus, but their heart is really in the world. Following Jesus has not impacted their life. For these, Jesus has comforted their guilty conscience, but not radically transformed how they live. For them, this life might be pretty easy. For those who choose to really surrender to the name of Jesus, to live by his morals and standards, they will come in direct opposition to the world. They will be hated. They may not be nailed to a cross, but they might lose their business. They might be called terrible things. They might lose a job. And in other parts of the world, they could lose their lives. Following Jesus is not for the faint of heart.

That's Not the End of the Story

If following Jesus puts everything I own, everything I have, and even my own life in jeopardy—why should I?

We are not standing at the end of history; we are standing in the middle of history. We are in the *meantime*. Something else is going to happen; something big—and it's going to change everything.

Jesus concluded his very strong words about what it means to follow him with what appears to be a very strange promise. He said that some of those who were with him as he spoke would not die until they saw him coming in his Kingdom. That would be a reference to the Second Coming.

When Jesus comes again, everything will change. He will reward those who faithfully served him and give them positions of great authority in his kingdom. They will gain everything. But those who stayed comfortable, compromised to the worlds value system and never truly followed Jesus, will lose everything.

How we live now, in the time between Jesus' first coming and his second coming, will greatly impact the rest of our eternity.

How Could they not die Before the Second Coming?

> *[T]here be some standing here, which shall not taste of death, till they see the Son of man coming in his kingdom.*
>
> — Matthew 16:28, KJV

Chapter 5—Transforming Power Of The Second Coming

Jesus' words seem impossible, don't they? In fact, it seems so impossible that Jesus could be referring to his Second Coming, that scholars come up with some outs for Jesus. Maybe he really means the resurrection. Or maybe he means Pentecost, when the Holy Spirit came down in power.

Three things about Matthew 16:28

1. Some will see Jesus *coming in his kingdom* within their own lifetime.
2. Even those who do see it will eventually die. Not taste death till they see... after that they may die.
3. Not all of those present are going to see it. *Some standing here.*

This seems to be speaking of Christ visible return to this earth. It is something they will see. And what a sight the coming will be! The Bible says the sky will open, the son of man will descend in glory, and the angels will go out across the earth to gather God's people to himself. There is a larger discussion within Christianity about if there is a rapture separate from the final coming. So, all cards are on the table, I believe there is only one coming of Jesus, referred to throughout Scripture as the *Parousia*—the *Coming*.

So, how could some see Jesus' Second Coming when it still hasn't happened? It seems time went on, Jesus did not come back, and they all died. Jesus' words are impossible, right?

The chronology of events can be hard to follow, even between the synoptic Gospels. But in all three, the Transfiguration is immediately after Jesus telling his disciples that some of them would not die until they saw the Son of man coming. The statement that some will see the Kingdom and the Transfiguration are locked together in all three Synoptics.

But the Transfiguration is not the Second Coming! Did Jesus make a mistake?

Peter himself helps us sort out what happened. What the disciples saw when they saw Jesus glorified at the Transfiguration was a preview of the Second Coming. They didn't see the whole thing. They didn't see the sky open, the angels descend, the saints gathered up. They saw one aspect of his Coming—HIM! They saw Jesus as he will be at his Second Coming.

The NIV translates Peter's description this way:

> We did not follow cleverly invented stories when we told you about the power and coming of our Lord Jesus Christ, but we were eyewitnesses of his majesty. For he received honor and glory from God the Father when the voice came to him from the Majestic Glory, saying, 'This is my Son, whom I love; with him I am well pleased.' We ourselves heard this voice that came from Heaven when we were with him on the sacred mountain.
>
> — 2 Peter 1:16-18

Peter says they were *eyewitnesses* of his majesty. Strong's Lexicon identifies *megaleiotes* as bearing the idea of *superbness* or *splendor*. Isn't that perfect? They saw his *superbness*!

The *coming* Peter is talking about is the same word so often used in connection with Jesus' Second Coming, *Parousia*.

To paraphrase Peter: *Look, we were not following a bunch of myths when we told you Jesus is coming again. We were there, and saw for ourselves, when he was on the mountain. And while we were on the mountain, we saw the majesty of the second coming for ourselves and we even heard the voice of God.*

Gnostics and others accused the apostles of making up the idea of a second coming. In their view, it was just a means of making sure Christians behaved. *Better be good, because Jesus is coming back. You don't want to be caught being bad.* But the apostles insisted they did not follow myths. They were not devising schemes to just keep people in line. They were true believers that a future was sure to occur.

While the second coming is something that is yet to happen, there is a sense in which the three apostles already saw it. They saw it ahead of time. Don't stress over this, time is not a problem for God.

I see it Already

A few years ago I took my daughters to Disneyland. I have four daughters, so I'm now broke. As we walked in, my daughter Susie said, "I don't feel good."

"Yes, you do," I said confidently.

"No, I really don't feel good."

I paused. "Listen, I paid a lot of money for you to have fun. And you're going to have fun."

Chapter 5—Transforming Power Of The Second Coming

"Can I ride on your shoulders then?" She asked.

I agreed. Big, bad mistake. Don't let someone who tells you that they don't feel good ride on your shoulders! Of course, you're smarter than me and surely already know what happened. As we walked through Disneyland—New Orleans Square specifically—my beloved child emptied her stomach on my head. Puke dripped from my hair, onto my clothes. It was nasty.

We took the child back to the hotel, where I cleaned up and my wife suggested I take the older girls over to the other park, *California Disney*. I'm not really a fan of that park, it's like Disneyland Junior—but she was offering to stay with the sick child, so I agreed.

As we walked around *California Disney*, I tried to find a ride my older kids would like.

"Let's ride THAT!" My daughter Sharon said, pointing at a ride called California Screamin'.

"Good deal," I said. "But just so you know up front, it has a loop."

She stared at the ride station, "No, it doesn't."

"Yes, it does."

She insisted, "No, dad, there's no loop. They don't have loops in Disneyland."

"First, you're not in Disneyland, you're in Disneyland Junior. Second, there is a loop."

And she did it again. "No, there's no loop."

Then I pointed. "Child, listen to me. I'm looking right at the loop! I know there's a loop because I can see it. With my eyes." I might have been cranky because of the puke incident an hour earlier, I don't know. But I knew there was a loop not because someone told me or because I read a brochure—I had seen it with my own eyes.

Peter becomes emphatic when discussing the coming of Jesus. His confidence in Jesus' return is not based on what others have said or even his own opinion—he already saw Jesus glorified. He had a personal viewing of a future event.

In his book *Miracles*, C.S. Lewis said this about the Transfiguration:

> The Transfiguration or *Metamorphosis* of Jesus is also, no doubt, an anticipatory glimpse of something to come.

Break New Ground With God

Douglas J. Moo, professor of New Testament at Trinity Evangelical Divinity School, writes in the *NIV Application Commentary*:

> As the name suggests, the Transfiguration involves a transformation in Jesus' appearance, but it is a transformation that reveals his true nature. It is this glorious and majestic nature, hidden, as it were, during his earthly life, that will be revealed to the entire world at the time of his return. Put simply, the Transfiguration reveals Jesus as the glorious King and Peter was there to see it. (p.75)

A while back there was a news article about a *Star Trek* fan named Daniel. Daniel was dying of cancer and only had weeks to live. He was really brokenhearted that he would not get to see the new film *Star Trek Into Darkness*. Weeks before the film came out, he went to a showing of *The Hobbit,* hoping to at least get to see the preview of the new *Star Trek* film. But once he got there, Daniel received some amazing news. He would not be watching *The Hobbit* but instead director J.J. Abrams had arranged for an exclusive screening of *Star Trek Into Darkness* just for Daniel and his family. They must truly have been excited.

Imagine the disciples excitement at seeing the glory in which Jesus will come, long before his second coming.

How is the Transfiguration like the Second Coming?

There are several ways in which the Transfiguration was almost a mirror of the things we will see at the Second Coming.

    1. Jesus' appearance in glory. Luke 9:29 tells us that his face was changed, and Matthew 17:2 says that his face shined *like the sun*. The Transfiguration was a preview of the Second Coming. They saw him as we will see him. They saw the Bridegroom ahead of time. When Jesus came incarnate through Mary's womb, he did not shine with the physical glory of God. One of the things often mentioned about his Second Coming is that he will come in great visible glory. In Matthew 16:27, before the three disciples saw the Transfiguration, he said that he was going to come in his Father's glory. Then, a few days later—they saw that very glory.

Jesus said in Matthew 24, that when he comes again the nations will see him coming in *great glory*. The KJV of Matthew 25:31 uses the word glory twice in one verse to describe his return:

When the Son of man shall come in his glory, and all the holy angels with him, then shall he sit upon the throne of his glory.

— Matthew 25:31, underlines mine

2. Presence of the cloud. Not only will his appearance be glorious, but note the presence of the cloud. Matthew 17:5 informs us that at the Transfiguration an unusual cloud came over the mountain. It is described in the Greek as *photeinos*. That is: *very bright*, or *well-illuminated*, or *lustrous*. John, in Revelation, said he saw this again. Note the importance of a white cloud:

Then I looked, and behold, a white cloud, and seated on the cloud one like a son of man, with a golden crown on his head, and a sharp sickle in his hand.

— Revelation 14:14, ESV

As mentioned earlier this cloud often accompanies appearances of God on earth. At the crossing of the Red Sea, at Mount Sinai, even when Solomon dedicated the temple, Yahweh came down in a cloud and the priest fled the presence of the Lord. The cloud is like a coat or robe, that covers the glory of God. As his inner glory shines, the cloud shrouds his visible presence. It is similar to the curtain of the Holy of Holies.

When Jesus comes again, he will come on the clouds. There are three possible reasons why this is significant. First, Jesus was physically raised from the dead. He dwells even now in a physical body. Yet, His physical body is not limited to the rules of this world. It is a sign of his being sovereign over all the world. Even in his resurrected physical body, he can ride on the clouds. Second, being seated in the clouds is a sign of honor given to God. Isaiah saw God where? Very high and lifted up. It is the cloud that shrouds his presence. Third, nothing can stop a cloud. With all our technology, we cannot control the clouds. In a similar way, we cannot stop the coming of Jesus.

3. Response of the disciples. A third way the Transfiguration is like the Second Coming is in the response of those who were nearby. When the disciples heard the voice of God speaking from the cloud, they fell on their faces. I think that will be our first response to

Break New Ground With God

the Second Coming. The Apostle Paul said in Philippians 2 that every knee will bow (see Philippians 2:10).

It's interesting to note the three locations Paul says the bowing will take place. First every knee will bow *in Heaven*. All of the believing dead will bow to Him. There was never anyone greater than Jesus. Moses, David, Solomon, and Jonah will all bow down to Jesus.

Also, every knee *on earth* will bow to Jesus. Believers and unbelievers alike will all fall to their knees in submission to the one true King. No one will be left standing,shaking their fist in God's face. Even the most devout ashiest will give up atheism on that day and bow down to Jesus. Christians, Hindu, Jews, Muslims, every religion will bow down. Every nation will bow down.

Paul says that those *under the earth* will bow down. This is a reference to hell. Imagine that! Across the landscape of the wicked, ungodly people will suddenly drop to their knees and begin shouting that Jesus is Lord. Imagine Satan, standing in disbelief as throngs of humans fall down and cry out, *"Jesus is Lord!"* "Stop that!" Satan shouts. But then another wave of humans drop to their knees. And just when it looks bad, it gets worse for the Tempter. Not only do humans bow down, but the demons begin to fall on their knees. Their wicked mouths—mouths that have done nothing but utter curses for eons, suddenly shout that Jesus is Lord. "YOU STOP THAT!" Satan demands. But just then, as if kicked from behind, Satan loses all the strength in his legs and falls to the ground. His mouth hangs open in surprise, and the arch enemy of Jesus Christ utters the words, *"Jesus is Lord."*

4. God speaks. Before moving on, there is one more way that the Transfiguration is like the Second Coming. Notice that at the Transfiguration, God the Father spoke down to planet earth. Don't breeze by that. God doesn't often speak with an audible voice from Heaven. According to Paul in Philippians 2, what causes all the bowing to take place is nothing short of the name of Jesus. It may be that when Christ comes again, God himself will utter his Sons name across the heavens and earth and even through the deepest pits of hell. Sure, he could have an angel do it—but could they reach so deep? Could angels carry the name to every ear all at once? Or could it be, much as at the Transfiguration, the Father himself will declare this the Son that he loves—Jesus—and like dominos every living being will fall down in submission?

Chapter 5—Transforming Power Of The Second Coming

An Ordinary Day

Jesus promised he would come again on an ordinary day. It would be like Noah's day—not because something spectacular happened the day before the flood. What was unique about the day before God flooded the earth was how normal everything seemed. People were still getting married, eating, drinking, going to funerals, rushing to work, buying in the market place, selling. There were wars, famines, and earthquakes. The normal events of life were rolling on. When suddenly, dramatically, God called it all to a stop with the first drop of rain. God flooded the world on a very ordinary day.

The Bible warns us that Jesus will bring an end to this time on an ordinary day.

> Two men will be in the field;
> one will be taken, one left.
> Two women will be grinding grain;
> one will be taken, one left.
> Two girls will be in the mall oohing over the latest fashion;
> one will be taken, one left.
> Two men will be watching a sporting event;
> one will be taken, one left.
> Two teens will the texting;
> one will be taken, one left.
> Two women will be watching children on a playground;
> one will be taken, one left.
> Two people will be sitting at church;
> one will be taken, one left.
> Two clerks will be ringing up customers;
> one will be taken, one left.
> Two students will be arguing theology;
> one will be taken, one left.
> Two tennis players will be playing tennis;
> one will be taken, one left.
> Two seniors will be comparing ailments;
> one will be taken, one left.
> Two preachers will be eating at a potluck;
> *both* will be taken.

It is exciting that some have already seen part of this unveiled for them. It's a reality we can anticipate.

When Jesus comes again, most of us imagine him making a downward descent. In Revelation 6:14, the Apostle John says that he saw the sky roll up like a scroll. In his book on 1-2 Thessalonians, G.K. Beale suggests that if John were writing today, he might describe it like a curtain being pulled back all at once. That is, suddenly the entire creation is ripped open and our physical reality will be invaded by the heavenly dimension that has always been nearby. Beale writes:

> When Christ appears, he will not descend from the sky over Boston or London or New York City or Hong Kong or any other localized area. When he appears, the present dimension will be ripped away, and Christ will be manifest to all eyes throughout the earth. (G.K. Beale, 1-2 Thessalonians, eBook)

Imagine suddenly all that we know and see will be dimmed by the glory all around us. On an ordinary day the dimensions of this world will be torn open, and Christ will pull those who belong to him into his arms. It will be splendid; it will be personal; it will be beautiful. That truth can change how we live right now.

Jesus is Coming—Soon

In Peter's second letter, he spends a great deal of time discussing Jesus' coming. Not only does he marvel at the fact he's already seen the glorified Jesus that we will see on that great day; Peter spends some time in chapter three discussing what that day will be like.

In 2 Peter 3:8, the apostle notes that it may seem like a long time before Jesus comes back. After all, a day for the Lord could be a thousand years! But there's a reason Jesus hasn't come back yet, and it's a very touching—because he loves us. Peter tells us that God in his patience has not brought final judgment on the earth because he wants everyone to have the opportunity to repent of sin and turn to God for salvation.

We should not assume God's patience means he is not coming. In fact, Peter says he will come like a thief. A thief doesn't call ahead and make arrangements! He just shows up unannounced. Peter says that on that day, the heavens themselves will disappear with a roar, the basic building blocks of creation will be melted down in a great fire and the planet itself will be stripped bare.

Jesus told us no one knows the day or the hour of his coming. No one. That includes the apostles who already saw his glory shining

Chapter 5—Transforming Power Of The Second Coming

from the future into their day; they didn't know how far away the future event was—and neither do we.

Of course, that hasn't stopped a slew of false prophets from suggesting they know when Jesus is coming back. In 1843, followers of William Miller sold their homes and businesses and went around preaching that Jesus was coming back the next year. As you know—he didn't.

Ellen G. White prophesied that Jesus actually had returned in 1844—but it was a spiritual coming, not a physical coming. Now to be clear, everything in the Bible speaks of a physical return of Jesus to this world. He will bring his physical resurrected body into this very real world and execute real judgment. There will be an audible trumpet—a visible Jesus shining in glory. Peter tells us the heavens will disappear with a roar. It'll be hard to miss.

Jesus' failure to return in 1844 didn't stop some from making new dates. Some suggested that 1844 was the beginning of the last generation on earth. They predicted Jesus would return in 1874.

In 1992 Harold Camping predicted Jesus would come back in 1994. That was my first year at California Baptist University. There I was, going to school, preparing for the future—totally unaware that the world was about to end. In fact, I'd just met a girl and was pretty sure for me the world was just beginning. Well, when 1994 didn't work out for Mr. Camping, he added 7 to his previous date and declared 2001 was the true coming of Jesus. Wrong again. So, he set a new date of May 21, 2011. His followers sold homes, gave out lots of bumper stickers and told the world the exact date of Jesus' coming. Only, Jesus didn't comply with their date setting. The date came and went, and Camping played an old trick. He said Jesus had in fact come back on May 21, but it was a spiritual coming. Sound familiar? The true date was yet to come.

Do we know when Jesus is coming back? We sure do—*soon!*

It will be unexpected—sudden. A day not predicted. In fact, I rather wish all these false prophets would stop giving out dates, because I rather think that just ensures the Lord will most defiantly not come on that date.

Jesus and Peter share the same message: The Lord will come in glory on a day no one expects. History will be interrupted. For many, it will be the worst day of their life. And for others, it will be the greatest day ever.

Break New Ground with God

The Transfiguration is recorded not only to bring home to us the glory of Jesus, but the sure reality of his Second Coming. It is a preview of Jesus' future glory.

The Second Coming has the power not only to transform tomorrow, but if you truly believe, it can transform you right now. That's because if we believe Jesus is coming again, it changes our behavior now.

As incredible as the coming of Jesus will be—Peter spends very little time on the details we get caught up in. We want to camp out on the details of Jesus' coming. Will he come on a horse? Will he descend to the Mount of Olives? Will the mountain split? What about the Millennial Kingdom?

In 2 Peter 3, as the apostle discusses the coming of Jesus, it is important to see that Peter is not worried about any of the minutia we want to focus on. He breaks away from the details like an old man looking up from a book. "You know, since everything is going to be destroyed like this, you better think about how you're living." He urges us in 2 Peter 3:14-15 to live lives that are spotless, blameless and at peace with God.

In other words: If you know Jesus is coming back, then it will change your behavior now. Faith isn't just thinking something real hard, it's believing it enough to let it change you.

Putting Truth into Action

If you are deliberately disobeying God, can you really say that you believe Jesus might come at any time? The truth is, if you are a believer living in sin, then you are hoping with all your heart Jesus doesn't come back! If you're sleeping with someone you're not married to, or endorsing something the Bible calls sin, or making immoral or unethical choices—those are big signs that your faith is suffering. Don't worry, you can fix it simply by making a choice.

Real faith takes guts. And you may have to swallow hard and make some tough decisions because of what you really believe.

If you believe we will one day answer to Jesus for how we live now, then you may have to have a face to face talk with someone you've been having sex with outside of marriage. "Hey, this has been a lot of fun, but it's killing my soul. This has to stop." At that moment, you will break new ground with God.

Chapter 5—Transforming Power Of The Second Coming

You might have to swallow hard and tell a friend, "That little scheme we've got going that's making us money. It's wrong, and I'm out." Boom! New ground broken.

You might have to have a talk with yourself. You know, the Bible says that Job said he made a covenant with his eyes not to look lustfully at a woman (see Job 31:1). And he had a wife who was difficult to say the least. But he didn't say, "Well, my wife has rejected me. And it's not adultery to look." No! He said, "Okay, self, I'm in a spot that could really lead me to serious temptation. So, listen up, eyes—we're not going to even look at a girl lustfully." Maybe you need to have that talk with yourself about a subject. Maybe it's porn or a perpetual sin.

Jesus said in Matthew 25 that the final exam involves how we treated the outcast, the poor, and those in prison. In other words, our faith is shown as genuine by how we treat those who are easily marginalized. After dealing with self and sin, our next step in faith is serving others.

Here's the amazing thing: As we make decisions based on faith, our faith muscle grows. You fall more in love with Jesus the more you honor him. So, what's hard at first, because it forces us to confront the flesh, becomes joyful. Soon you're glad you got out of that immorality or changed that behavior, because you feel the Master's happiness. And as you make changes, you no longer dread the return of the Lord, you look forward to seeing his glory. That same glory Peter, James, and John saw two thousand years ago.

When Jesus comes again, there will be two groups. The "OH NO!" group. They are broken hearted that they did not serve him while there was time. And the "OH YEAH!" group. They look up and see the glory of Jesus and know that eternity is going to be great. Peter encourages us to live so that we can look forward to his coming.

Digging Deeper

Take a moment to reflect on some things you would do if you knew Jesus was coming back in one year.

1. How does believing in the Coming of Jesus transform your daily decisions?

   _____
   _____

2. Do you look forward to the Coming of Jesus, or is it something you quietly dread?

   _____
   _____

3. Do you find it difficult to really believe Jesus will come again? What are some things that impede your faith when it comes to the Second Coming?

   _____
   _____

4. If you were going on a great trip, you'd tell a lot of people. You'd be really excited. Have your shared with friends and family how excited you are about Christ coming?

   [ ] Yes   [ ] No

5. I suggested in this section that there are two groups when it comes to the Second Coming; the OH NO group and the OH YEAH group. Which camp will most of your friends be in?

   [ ] Oh No   [ ] Oh Yeah

Chapter 5—Transforming Power Of The Second Coming

6. If you have children, have you shared with them the truth of the Second Coming? How did they respond?

    [ ] Yes   [ ] No

    _____
    _____

7. When you think about the Second Coming, what are some things you are looking forward to? Here's a few of mine—feel free to join me or write your own.

    [ ] Rising up to meet Jesus in the air.
    [ ] Hearing all creation declare Jesus is Lord.
    [ ] Seeing Jesus' face.
    [ ] Being instantly transformed.
    [ ] Seeing the dead raised.
    [ ] Flying.
    [ ] Hearing the trumpet.
    [ ] Feeling his hand wipe away painful tears.
    [ ] _____
    [ ] _____
    [ ] _____
    [ ] _____

8. What are some things you are not looking forward to about the Second Coming?

    _____
    _____
    _____

9. Who do *you* say Jesus is?

    _____
    _____

6 Why Listening To Jesus Is Painful

The LORD your God will raise up for you a prophet like me from among your own brothers. You must listen to him.
Deuteronomy 18:15

Wouldn't it be great to hear Jesus preach? The wind softly blowing as the Master's voice rises and falls from the hillside.

When people heard Jesus teach, they came away amazed. They said no one spoke like that, with real authority (see Matthew 7:28-29). It was like God himself had come down to earth and started teaching! Which, of course, is exactly what happened.

Truth #4
God's Word must be read for truth, not just for comfort

But beyond amazement, actually listening to Jesus can be a little difficult. Maybe even painful.

After all, if it was easy to listen to Jesus, then we wouldn't need God to tell us to *listen to him*. Think about that! How many times has God actually spoken from Heaven to people living on earth in an audible voice? Not often. When God speaks out loud—not just to our heart, but in a real voice—it's going to be something that's a big deal.

What would you expect God to say?

This is my son—that's pretty important stuff. That cuts to the heart of the Trinity and person of Jesus. God wanted us to know the identity of Jesus. This was so important that God did not leave it for us to debate and guess. He wanted us to know that Jesus is the Son of God.

Wouldn't it be nice if the next thing the voice from Heaven told us was about predestination, or the secrets of Noah's ark? But God said something that seems obvious—*we should listen to Jesus.*

Why would God need to tell us that? Why not skip the obvious and tell us some secret or new revelation?

Probably because we don't really listen to Jesus. In fact, the truth is, Jesus says a lot of painful things. On the surface, all seems fine. But when you really listen to what Jesus is saying, he tends to offend our modern ears. He tells us things like—*love your enemies.* Is he serious? Well according to the voice from Heaven, he's very serious!

Often, we listen to the stuff from Jesus that we want to hear. We operate with selective hearing. Thus, God does the incredible act of speaking from a cloud to three apostles to make it very clear—God wants us to deeply listen to Jesus.

God Spoke to Moses

Standing on the Mount of Transfiguration with Jesus is the Law Giver, Moses. The command to listen to Jesus seems to validate something God told Moses in Deuteronomy 18:15. The Lord promised that he would raise up a prophet in the future.

God told Moses that when they came into the Promised Land, the people there have given their ear to those who are practicing sorcery and divination. God would raise up a prophet from among the Hebrews—not a Gentile—who would speak God's Word to the people. God's specific command, *"You must listen to him"* (Deuteronomy 18:15).

God's voice and the presence of Moses, both stand to confirm that the promise has now been fulfilled—Jesus stands in the role of the prophet promised by God.

God Spoke on Mount Sinai

After telling Moses that the people must listen to the Prophet, God reminded him of the events on Mount Horeb (Sinai) recorded in Exodus 19. Something amazing was about to happen—God was going to speak from the mountain to the people. Talk about a message you want to hear!

God told Moses that before he spoke to the people, he wanted them to promise they would obey him. After a series of promises, Moses went back and assured Yahweh that the people did indeed in-

Chapter 6—Why Listening To Jesus Is Painful

tend to obey God. Moses then instructed the people to prepare themselves to hear from God. They were to get themselves spiritually right. God instructed them to wash their clothes. God did not even want the dirt of the world to stain his people as they stood before him. They were not even to have sexual relations with their spouses because God wanted them to be fully focused on their relationship with him, not one another.

This was a big deal. God was about to speak. They even put barriers around the mountain so that no one could climb into the presence of God. The entire mountain was about to become a holy site, and the people were about to hear the voice of God.

When God comes down on the mountain, it is an amazing moment. There is thunder, lighting, and (get this!) a thick cloud descends on the mountain as a trumpet blast. There's that cloud again, shrouding the *Shekinah* of God. Notice also that there is a trumpet blast. God physically descended from Heaven to the mountain top. The Bible says that the mountain began to smoke because God had descended on the mountain *in fire*. The mountain *trembles* violently as if it might not be able to bear the weight of God's throne. Naturally, the people are terrified. Moses then led the people from their camp to the foot of the mountain.

When the Hebrews standing at the foot of the mountain heard the thunder, and the trumpet, and saw the lighting, they were terrified. As they stood in front of the mountain, the earth quaking and sky flashing with light as the mountain blazed; they were suddenly afraid that if they did hear God speak they would die.

The people did not want to hear God's voice directly; they wanted a prophet to stand between them and God. That would become the role of Moses. Over and over Moses would climb the mountain, speak to God, then deliver God's word back to the people. The people could have heard directly from God; but they wimped out! It was too much for them to bear. Apparently, listening to God took guts.

In Deuteronomy 18, God told Moses that he had not fully given up on speaking to the people directly. In fact, God would raise up another prophet, and the people were to listen to him. Though Moses did not fully understand it then, God was referring to Jesus.

Jesus is not only a prophet; he is God in flesh. But he fulfills the prophecy of Deuteronomy 18 by carrying God's Word directly to God's people.

Moses testified in Deuteronomy 18:17 that Yahweh told him what the people asked for was good. In fact, God would send them a prophet, and he would put his words in the prophet's mouth. But there was a warning. If anyone chose to ignore the words of the prophet, then God would discipline them. And worse, if any prophet should come along and claim to speak for God, but say things God had not commanded—the punishment would be death. In other words, claiming to speak on behalf of God is a really big deal.

On the Mount of Transfiguration, when God said, "*Listen to him,*" he confirmed that Jesus was the prophet he had promised long ago. He was the One who would have God's words in his mouth.

He did this with Moses, the one to whom he had made the promise, physically present. Moses stood on the mountain that day bearing witness that Jesus is God's promised Prophet who would deliver God's Word to us directly. When Jesus speaks, it is just as powerful as God speaking from Mount Sinai. Why does God need to tell us to listen to Jesus? Because he need say no more! Once he has told us to listen to Jesus, Jesus himself now has the mike and speaks God's Word to us.

Allow Jesus to Offend You

John 6 records that Jesus fed a multitude. That was a great attention getter. In fact, people began to discuss running Jesus for public office. This guy should be King, they said. After all, a leader who could multiply bread could keep them all satisfied. But Jesus was not at all interested in running for political office. He knew that they just wanted a bread machine; a perpetual cafeteria; they were looking for Home Town Buffet; they wanted full stomachs, not a King to rule their hearts.

Later, when they all showed up at a Synagogue, Jesus told them they had to *eat his flesh and drink his blood*. Strange, right? Stunned by this, many people start getting uncomfortable. Does that cause Jesus to back off? No way. He keeps saying it! And they can't figure out what he means by *eat his flesh and drink his blood*. The conversation gets so intense, the Jews began to quarrel with each other about what he meant.

How could Jesus ask them to *eat his flesh*? Does that stop Jesus? Not at all. He presses it even further, telling them that unless they *eat his flesh and drink his blood*, they will not have life. Jesus then

Chapter 6—Why Listening To Jesus Is Painful

gives them a promise: Those who do in fact *eat his flesh and drink his blood* will be *raised up on the last day*. By the time he tells them this, people are getting seriously disturbed. Does that stop Jesus? No, it doesn't! Jesus tells them that his *flesh* is real food, and his *blood* is real drink.

Are you picturing a dumbfounded group of Israelites? Don't get judgmental: you would have been totally confused, too. No one at this point is taking sermon notes and filling in the blanks. Everyone's mouth is just hanging open in disbelief. Does that stop Jesus? No. He goes on.

Probably, the more Jesus said that day, the more the crowd thinned. Finally, the Bible tells us that many of those following him said something startling.

This is a hard saying; who can listen to it?

— John 6:60, ESV

Read that again! What did God tell Moses we must do when he sends the prophet? *"Listen to him"* (Deuteronomy 18:19). What did the voice from the cloud tell them? *"Listen to him"* (Mark 9:7).

What did they not do? They did not listen to him. Why? Because Jesus was confusing them. Worse, he was offending them. He offended their culture, their understanding of Scripture and their own personal faith. Rather than continue to be offended, many chose to walk away that day.

Here is a really tough question. Do you have a faith strong enough to bear the offense of Jesus? Have you ever dared to allow Jesus to offend you? Or do you demand God only speak comforting, kind, easy things to you? If you have never had God wound you; never had him hurt you and offend you—your faith hasn't had opportunity to grow very deep yet.

Here's the truth: if you really hear God speak, he's going to challenge you. He's going to challenge your theology; he's going to challenge your own ideas; he's going to challenge your assumptions and even your world view. He might challenge your political leanings and your deeply held opinions. Does it upset you to know that Jesus isn't bothered when we're offended? He probably even expects it.

I'm surprised when people boldly tell God what they want to hear. "Lord, give us a word of _____" fill in the blank—praise, hope, encouragement, knowledge.

I'm sure God does speak all those things; but maybe we should just come and simply ask for his Word. Have you ever heard anyone pray, "Lord, give me a word of correction!" or, "Lord, discipline me. I'm open to your chastening."?

What would happen in your faith if you said, "Jesus Christ, I really want to hear you. Even if you wound me, hearing you is more important to me than anything else." If you did, God would begin leading you in a very personal way like never before.

No Where Else to Go

In John 6, many people decided they did not want to listen to Jesus. In Deuteronomy 18 God told Moses:

> *If anyone does not listen to my words that the prophet speaks in my name, I myself will call him to account.*
>
> — Deuteronomy 18:19

The people didn't want to hear God on Mount Sinai. So, God himself (Jesus) came down to deliver his Word. Not in thunder on a shaking mountain, but clothed in human skin. And know what? They still rejected him. People still walked away, angry and confused and disappointed. Jesus did not say the things they wanted to hear.

As the crowd thinned, Jesus got wind of the complaining among his disciples. *"Are you offended?"* He asked them. He's stunned at how sensitive they are. Then he said something that really perplexed them. *"Just suppose you saw me ascend to where I was before."*

In other words, "Not long ago, I sat on the throne above all Creation. If you understood who was talking to you, then you would listen very closely to me. You'd hang on my every word."

With that, a final great wave of disciples leave Jesus. Andy Stanley says they *un-followed* him. They walked away. He has cut his listening crowd from something like five thousand, to twelve. Then Jesus does something unexpected; he turns to the twelve remaining and asks them if *they* also would like to *un-follow* him.

The truth is, many of us will consider walking away from Jesus because his words do not conform to what we want to hear.

Chapter 6—Why Listening To Jesus Is Painful

The hardest thing for me as a pastor is not doing funerals or even administrating a church; it's speaking honest truth to people who say they follow Jesus but make lifestyle choices that do not conform to God's Word.

- How can you say you follow Jesus, but you're choosing this lifestyle?
- How can you claim Jesus is your Lord, but you treat your wife like this?
- How can you say Jesus is your Lord, but you keep moving from one relation to another?
- How can you sing praises to Jesus' name, and refuse to talk to your mother? Don't you remember that Jesus said we're supposed to honor our father and mother?
- How can you publicly claim to love Jesus, but your mouth is full of curses? Don't you know that Jesus said out of the overflow of the heart the mouth speaks?

Those are difficult conversations because I know that as I speak, the person is quietly thinking about if this is the point where they might choose to *un-follow*. Or at least find a church and a pastor who will not quote the parts of the Bible that makes them uncomfortable.

Jesus understood his teaching was difficult. The Hebrews at Mount Sinai were frightened away from truly listening to God because of the thunder, lightning and fire that came from the mountain. God's majesty terrified them. If God's presence came with such power, they were sure God's voice would kill them. So, God turned down the volume to make his teaching very clear. When God's Son came down, he did not come with thunder, lightning, or fire. It was just Jesus, simply declaring God's Word. But it was still more than people could bear. They were not offended by the thunder, lightning, and power of God—they were offended by his words.

When Jesus offered the disciples the opportunity to leave—to un-follow—Peter spoke up for the disciples by asking Jesus a question.

> *Lord, to whom shall we go? You have the words of eternal life, and we have believed, and have come to know that you are the Holy One of God.*
>
> — John 6:68-69, ESV

> ### Peter Affirmed Three Things
> 1. No one else is going to say the things Jesus says. We may not always like it, but we need it.
> 2. Jesus is the one they were waiting for. Peter acknowledges that Jesus is the *Christ*. He is the expected Messiah. Jesus is *The Prophet* who was to bring them God's Word.
> 3. Finally, Peter notes that not only does he believe Jesus is the Messiah, but he is the Son of God. He bears a unique relationship to the Father that no one else can obtain.

In other words, Peter says, "No, we're not leaving. Not because we're always comfortable with the things you say, because we're not. Jesus, you often make us uncomfortable. But we believe there's no one else like you. So, if we leave you, no one else is going to give us what you have to give us."

Putting Truth into Action

Why is it so hard to listen to Jesus? Why would God need to tell us to listen to him? Why does he bother us so much?

Jesus takes the Word of God and applies it directly to us. And it hurts.

My wife and I love the musical, *The Phantom of the Opera*. I recently found a company that offers a *Personalized* edition of Gaston Leroux's novel. They reprint the novel with your loved ones names as key characters. That's what Jesus did to the Bible. He put our names and inner struggles into it. He personalized the scriptures.

When it comes to the Bible, application is painful. God gave his Word on Mount Sinai through Moses. But instead of taking it in deeply and personalizing it, the people turned it into a series of ceremonies and rules. So, long as God's Word could be kept at a *do* and *do-not* list, then the heart didn't get overly involved. But Jesus took the Word of God and carried it into the sanctuary of our hearts.

I can just imagine a conversation with Jesus something like this.

> Jesus: *You heard you shouldn't commit adultery, right?*
>
> Self: Yep, I heard it. So far, so good. Haven't slept with any woman I'm not married to lately.

Chapter 6—Why Listening To Jesus Is Painful

Jesus: *Good. But I don't just want you to physically keep the command. I want you to keep the command in your heart. It has to go to the core of who you are. In fact, if you even look lustfully at a woman, you've committed adultery in your heart.*

Self: No response!

When we encounter truth that radical, our mind starts racing:

"I don't like that! That pretty much makes all men with eyes serial adulterers. I'm not a fan of being called an adulterer. I don't like someone accusing me of that. In fact, that whole thing is pretty uncomfortable, and it feels unfair. I haven't committed adultery! Why is Jesus guilting me over this?"

Jesus would remind us that God told Moses on Mount Sinai that we can't kill each other. Murder is out. And most of us feel pretty good on that one—until we have Jesus come apply it to our lives. Jesus would insist that if we hate someone, we've committed murder in our hearts. That's brutal!

A thriving faith welcomes God's inspection and correction. A faith that is strong is a faith that anticipates not only God's comfort through the Scriptures, but his forceful direction. If we want to be people of faith, we have to ask God to take his Word and show us how it applies deeply to us. And the result will at first be very uncomfortable.

You may not like how God applies his Word in relation to your attitude toward your mother-in-law. You may not enjoy the way God shows you how his Word speaks to the way you treat your boss or those in authority over you. In so many situations, you're probably not going to like the way Jesus applies God's Word to your life. Yet, a person of faith will say, "This is exactly what I need! Lord, please don't stop."

Often Jesus would say, *"He who has ears to hear, let him hear!"* He meant our spiritual ears. Ears that are willing to listen to the truth, even when we want to cover them and ignore everything he is saying, because it is so different from the way we want things to be.

Digging Deeper

1. Has anyone ever offended you, then you realized they were right?

    [ ] Yes   [ ] No

2. Take a moment and list some offensive things Jesus said to the people of his day.

    _____
    _____
    _____
    _____

3. Has God, the Bible, or the words of Jesus ever offended or bothered you?

    _____
    _____
    _____
    _____

4. Struggling with a passage of Scripture can cause great breakthroughs with God. Has there ever been a time when you really struggled to understand a passage, or come to terms with something the Bible said, and the result was a great breakthrough in your walk with God?

    _____
    _____
    _____
    _____

Chapter 6—Why Listening To Jesus Is Painful

5. At our church's new members class, I share my "least favorite" Bible verse. I share this to make it clear that even if we don't like it, it's still true. My liking or not liking something the Bible says does not affect its truthfulness. Do you have a least favorite Bible verse? *Mine is James 4:17.* It's good to know your least favorite verse so that you will be mindful not to ignore it just because you don't like it.

   _____

6. Has there ever been a time you found it very difficult to listen for God's voice in a situation? Maybe it was a time when…
   - [ ] You already knew what you wanted the answer to be.
   - [ ] You did not like what the Bible said.
   - [ ] You were angry and wanted to lash out at someone.
   - [ ] The demands of Scripture seemed unfair for the situation you were in.

7. What passage(s) of Scripture has God used to profoundly touch your walk with him?

   _____

   _____

   _____

8. Okay: what's your favorite Bible verse(s)?

   _____

   _____

   _____

7 Rethink How You Read The Bible

> *Now the Bereans were of more noble character than the Thessalonians, for they received the message with great eagerness and examined the Scriptures every day to see if what Paul said was true.*
> Acts 17:11

How we read the Bible matters. A dear friend of mine named Doris used to encourage me as I preached. Doris, an African-American woman, would give a solid, "Amen!" when she thought I'd driven a point home. "Preach it!" she would say sometimes. And, when something from the Word of God really hurt, she would shake her head and say, "Well now, you're just meddling." It was funny, and she meant it to be. What she was saying was—it's getting personal. The Bible is getting in my space.

In this chapter, we will be digging deeper into Truth #4—*God's Word must be read for truth, not just comfort.*

Stop Reading the Bible that Way

Some of you need to stop reading the Bible the way you're reading it. Notice I said some of you. Not all—y'all. Just, if the shoe fits.

Stop telling God ahead of time what you want the Bible to tell you. For example, those who open it and say, "God, encourage me today." And some who take their Bible and say, "Now Lord, I really need a word today about prosperity." And, "Lord, would you give me a word today about wealth."

If you go to the Word declaring what you desire to hear, you are deciding ahead of time to pick and choose what you find there.

A man in our church sent me an email titled, "Why highly successful people start their day reading the Bible."

I replied to the email as follows:

The reason to read the Bible is not to be highly successful—it's to know God. The reason to know God is not to be highly successful. Our King lost all his friends, had no money, no place to rest his head, was crucified, and said to us—if you love me, don't think you'll be treated different than me. I'm not against success, I'm concerned when we are more interested in success than knowing God. When we think knowing God is the path to success instead of the path to eternal life. When we have success, our question should be: God, how do you want me to expend and use my influence for you?

When we turn God's Word into short statements that are nothing more than Facebook memes, we miss the thrust of Scripture. It's like we live life immersed in Bible verses that are missing their context. There are stores with verses on mugs, jars, signs, shoes, bracelets, headbands, socks (I'm not kidding), and more. But often the verses we choose, when standing alone, don't say what they say when standing with the words around them. What we are doing is taking the stuff we really like, the one-liners, and plastering them all over the place. Sometimes even changing their meaning. Meanwhile, we are quietly hoping no one asks us about Romans 1:18. You just looked up Romans 1:18, didn't you?

While God's Word does comfort us, it was given to confront and change us. The truth, though often painful, is ultimately more comforting than a soothing lie.

If you read the Bible only for encouragement, to empower yourself and motivate you for the day—you're reading it wrong. We are to approach the Bible saying, "Jesus Christ, I want to listen to you. What do you want to show me? Where do you want to correct me?" God might show you things you didn't want to see. He might show you passages you've never heard in a sermon, because pastors were scared to talk about the content.

Do we Need to Amend the Bible?

On Christmas Eve, 2012, Pierce Morgan interviewed Dr. Rick Warren, pastor of Saddleback Church. The discussion focused on gay marriage. When Warren stated that he believed in a Biblical definition of marriage, Morgan declared that he believed the Bible is basically *inherently flawed* and that it is time to *amend* the Bible.

Dr. Warren responded, "Opinion changes, but truth doesn't."

Chapter 7—Rethink How You Read The Bible

We live in a culture that would like to rewrite the Bible. And even in the modern church, many Christians stand only by Scriptures they personally agree with. That is, the truth is now defined by their conscience, not by what God says is true. That's popular, but it's spiritual cyanide.

When we read and quote the Bible in a way that keeps us safe, politically correct, socially comfortable, and personally popular—we fail to truly engage with God. It empties us of the ability to move forward in our faith.

Augustine of Hippo said:

> If you believe what you like in the Gospel, and reject what you don't like, it is not the Gospel you believe, but yourself.

Violent Scripture Reading

Engaging with God's Word is serious business. This might surprise you, but when you really dig into what God wants from you, there's going to be some blood left on the ground. It will either be yours, or the prophets. (I'm speaking metaphorically. Someone is going to suggest I'm actually saying you kill the prophets.)

Here's what I do mean: Sometimes the Bible offends us. Sometimes God's Word makes us angry. Just have a talk in today's society about the Bible's definition of marriage. Suddenly there's blood. People are angry with God's Word because it will not conform to our cultural norms. In fact, the Bible will contradict culture. In many cases, instead of obeying the Bible, people do violence to the Word of God.

Jesus said in Matthew 11 that John the Baptist was the greatest man ever born. And then he added this interesting note:

> *From the days of John the Baptist until now the Kingdom of Heaven has suffered violence, and the violent take it by force.*
>
> — Matthew 11:12, ESV

Violent men do violence to God's Kingdom. How? By using God's Word, and God's Kingdom, and God's program, and God's movement for their own cause. They attempt to turn what belongs to God—God's Kingdom—into their Kingdom.

We do that when we take that which belongs to God, His Word, and manipulate it to say what comforts us instead of allowing it to confront us. To misuse the Bible is to do violence to God's Kingdom.

To teach something the Bible does not teach misrepresents the very nature of God.

To truly struggle with Scripture though, will leave us personally bloodied. The Bible will stab at our opinions, cut down our attitudes, and make great demands of us.

As Jesus and the disciples came down the mountain, Jesus *commanded* them not to tell anyone what they had seen until after the resurrection. This prompted the disciples to ask Jesus, "*Why do the scribes say that first Elijah must come?*" (Mark 9:11). If Jesus was indeed the Christ, had Elijah come and they missed it? Or, perhaps they are asking if what they just experienced was the coming of Elijah. Jesus responded by affirming that Elijah would indeed come first. Then he surprised them—Elijah had come! His name was John the Baptist.

How could John the Baptist be Elijah? Because Jesus clarified that it was not Elijah himself who must come first, but the office or role of Elijah would precede the coming of the Messiah.

John came preaching the truth, and people didn't like it. Just like they didn't like Elijah's preaching! John boldly confronted King Herod, and Herod's wife hated him for that. John was thrown in prison, and ultimately at the finagling of his wife, John was executed by beheading. There was blood on the ground over the Word of God.

You may not kill someone because you don't like what the Bible says, but in a sense when we reject God's Word we leave blood on the ground. But when we accept God's Word, when we allow it to cut us, the changes it can make are powerful and dramatic.

The great danger of modern Christianity is our belief that doctrine doesn't matter. We value sincerity of faith over digging for truth. God wants us sincere, but it can't stop there. It takes courage today to say, "I'm not just going to believe whatever I want. I'm going to let the Bible define my beliefs."

Many people assume God is like them. Thus, they don't feel they need the Bible to tell them about God—they figure God is using their moral compass. They have it completely backward. God is not at all like us. God is totally different than us. We cannot just believe what we want and make our own moral compass god. We must do violence to our moral compass, because it's wrong. We must reset our entire being to God's truth, as revealed in His Word, as our true North Star.

Chapter 7—Rethink How You Read The Bible

The Bible will Personally Confront You

My father, who pastored for many years, once encountered a situation where some serious lies about someone were spreading through the church. After asking some questions of various people in the church, he discovered one woman was at the center of the lies. She was sharing her opinion about someone with other women in the church, and the damage was very painful.

Dad confronted the woman and explained that she absolutely could not continue to spread gossip. Her response was stunning. "It's okay, this is the way women are. Women talk this way," she said.

"It doesn't matter how women normally talk. This is not the way the Bible commands us to behave," dad responded.

His urging for Biblical obedience resulted in her leaving the church angry. Who was he to tell her to obey the Bible? She certainly had Bible verses she was comfortable with on her walls and carried a Bible to church. But when the Bible offered true resistance to her behavior, she retreated to natural instinct.

Here's the problem: when we fail to apply God's Word to our heart, we are getting the Bible wrong. And if we get the Bible wrong, no transformation can take place. The adulterer remains in adultery with no one calling him to a higher standard. The gossip remains a gossip. The liar remains a liar. But when the Bible is used not only for our comfort but as our standard of truth, it has the power to open our eyes and give us enormous spiritual breakthroughs.

Gotta get it Right

If we get the Bible wrong, if we get the voice of Jesus wrong—we're going to mess life up. And worse, we're going to mess up other people's lives.

To bungle God's Word is not just personally dangerous—it's dangerous to the people around you. It's disastrous to your kids and your family and your church. If you mess up truth and just tell people comforting things they want to hear, you might be popular, but the Bible has another word for that—false teacher. A false teacher ascribes something to God that did not come from God.

In Pisa, Italy there's a tower that leans. Ever heard of it? The top of the tower is twelve feet from where it should be if the tower stood straight. The tower could also be called the sinking tower, because the entire thing began to sink into the ground when the third floor was constructed. It took 177 years to build the tower with 1,272 workers. They tried to compensate for the tilt by building the upper floors with one side taller than the other. It worked; only then the tower shifted and leaned the other direction.

All because the tower sits on a bad foundation. I know this: I don't want to lay a sloppy spiritual foundation for those around me. Even if I must dig a little deeper, work a little harder—I want to get the Bible right.

Why do you believe what you believe? What is your foundation in life? Some believe out of tradition. It's what their parents believed, and grandparents and culture, but it is not personal. The result of tradition as a standard of truth is that it does not truly move us closer to God. It does not break any new ground. Some believe out of aspiration. They aspire what they believe to be true. They're hoping it's right because it feels right.

Faith that really breaks new ground is faith that is born of conviction. You heard the Gospel, and at your core you knew it was true. You may have studied it, as the Bereans did (see Acts 17:11). The Apostle Paul wrote to the Thessalonians:

> *Our gospel came to you not simply with words, but also with power, with the Holy Spirit and with deep conviction.*
>
> *— 1 Thessalonians 1:5*

They didn't just aspire it to be true; it certainly was not their tradition or culture—they believed because the Holy Spirit convicted with power. God's truth was enough to cause them to turn from idols and build on a firm foundation.

A person of faith does not trust their own moral compass, that's a foundation that will cause the entire structure of life to lean; they look to God and his Word to direct their decision making.

Putting Truth into Action

If you really want to listen to Jesus, you might have to radically change how you approach God's Word.

You will probably not be invited to the foot of a mountain where God himself will come down and speak to you in an audible voice. So, how are we supposed to listen to Jesus? Hearing Jesus speak to us involves the following key elements.

Chapter 7—Rethink How You Read The Bible

1. Read the Bible habitually. To hear the Lord speak and discern his voice, we must be very familiar with God's written word. This is because God speaks from his Word, and he will never contradict the written word. Having a strong grasp on what God has already said in the Bible is very important to knowing what he is saying to you personally.

2. Tell God you're listening. In 1 Samuel 3, the boy Samuel worked for the leader of his nation, Eli. One night, as Samuel slept, God called to him, "*Samuel.*" Young Samuel jumped up and asked Eli what he wanted. But Eli hadn't said a word to him. That happened two more times before Eli gave him this advice: Next time he calls you, say, "*Speak, Lord, your servant is listening.*"

You might follow Eli's advice and tell God up front, "God, I'm your *servant*, and I want to hear you. Please speak to me."

3. Ask God to show you how the Bible applies to your life. As you read God's Word, you should be bold enough to tell God, "Lord, even if you must wound me, I am interested in what you have to say."

Sometimes God will bring a verse to mind long after you read it. One day I was really hurting over some hurtful things a family in our church had done. I had been very close to this family, and I felt personally attacked and betrayed. I learned about things they said about me to others, and the hurt just went deeper. Ultimately our church had to fulfill Jesus' command in Matthew 18 and remove them from the church fellowship. Years after those events unfolded, the memories were still painful. And I would wonder, what could have been? What if things had played out differently? And one day God spoke deeply to my heart, "David (me, not King David), *how long will you mourn for Saul?*" In other words, there were new things God wanted to do, but I was spending my time looking at hurts from the past.

Because I knew the Scripture from 1 Samuel 16:1, God was able to speak it to my heart at a crucial moment. He was able to confront my sinful anger toward those who hurt me and redirect my thinking.

Prayerfully asking Jesus to apply his word to us is a powerful step toward hearing God's voice. It tells God in advance—I am willing to hear you even if I don't like what you say.

Break New Ground With God

4. Wrestle with Scriptures you are not comfortable with. Yes, you read that right. Sometimes reading the Bible can be like a wrestling match. Sometimes we will struggle with what it says, what it means and how it applies. There are some scriptures we wrestle with before we find peace. Maybe you don't like what God says about divorce and remarriage. Instead of ignoring what Jesus said, I would encourage you to engage with him all the more on that text. Study it, think on it and pray it out.

Wrestling with the Bible means that we do not just take pat answers and move along. We become very interested in exactly what the Bible really means to say to us. What does Paul mean when he says a deacon must be the husband of one wife? What does Jesus mean when he says a branch that doesn't produce fruit will be cut away? We may feel we have an answer we like, but are we sure it's true? Instead of just being comfortable with the text, how willing have we been to fully engage with it? To think past our own traditions, opinions—even our favorite teachers—in order to seek exactly what God's Word is.

5. Listen often to Godly teachers. It's important for all of us to listen to others teach God's Word. God will often speak clearly through gifted preachers and teachers. He will use them to encourage us from the word, confront us and teach us. God will give us insights we would have never found on our own through others.

One reason it's important to listen to others is because they will say things that are true and apply directly to us. These might be things God has been trying to show us for a long time, but we find little ways of not giving him our attention in that area. Sometimes we are ignoring God, and it takes a teacher to come along and say, "Hey, look right there! This is what that means." And in our heart, the Lord leaps, "Yes! Listen to him! You've been ignoring me on this for a long time!"

6. Engaging others. I think one of the healthiest things we can do is invite other mature believers into our struggle with Scripture. As you think through and wrestle with a text, you hopefully start talking to others about how they understand that text. You are inviting them onto the mat with you. Often, they will see things from a vantage point you didn't have; or they will have an insight from life experience that you would have missed out on if you hadn't sought their thoughts. Often the best place to engage with others in God's Word is in Bible study.

Jesus promised that his sheep—those who belong to him—would hear his voice. Even when it is painful, for a true believer, it is always a joyful thing to be aware that God has spoken to you.

7. Pre-Decide. God directs us out of his love. He wants us to respond in love. Obedience is love for God. In John 14, Jesus very clearly says over and over in rapid fire that those who love him are those who obey him. In John 14:15, he said that if we really love him we would obey his commands. Then six verses later (John 14:21), he reminded us that those who keep his commandments are the ones who love him. Two verses after that, Jesus said that those who love him are those who keep his word. In the next verse, Jesus explained it in the reverse, saying that those who do not obey him are those who do not love him.

To be clear: obedience is the way we display our love toward God. And disobedience is an act of un-love toward Jesus.

I encourage you to open your Bible and tell God, "God, whatever you are about to show me: I'm going to obey you."

But shouldn't we do that after God shows us what he wants us to do? I don't think so.

Let me share with you what doesn't work; when we treat God's Word as if it is one of many sources of possible truths (our conscience, the world around us, friends and family.) That attitude dilutes the power of God's Word, treating the Almighty as if he is just one of many sources of direction. God is not willing to play second fiddle to anyone. He wants our full attention and our full obedience. A faithful person will commit to God before God even says what he wants. If we want to hear Jesus speak to us, it is vital we commit to obeying him before we even read and discover what he wants from us.

Lord, whatever you want, whatever you reveal to me, I choose today to obey you. That's a powerful prayer.

Digging Deeper

1. Is there a wrong way to read the Bible?

    [ ] Yes   [ ] No

2. What are some things you believe only because you believe the Bible is God's Word?

    _____

    _____

3. Has the Bible ever offended you?

    [ ] Yes   [ ] No

4. If you could amend something in the Bible, what would it be? (This is helpful to think about so you can know what portions of Scripture you might be tempted to ignore or lighten.)

    _____

    _____

5. What verse is often misused in your circles?

    _____

    _____

6. Have you ever felt God directly comfort you through the words of Scripture?

    [ ] Yes   [ ] No

7. Is there a text in Scripture that you have really wrestled with that made you uncomfortable?

    [ ] Yes   [ ] No

Chapter 7—Rethink How You Read The Bible

8. We looked at seven key elements that will help us approach God's Word for Spiritual breakthroughs. Which of the six is an area you need to focus on in the next 3 days?

    [ ] Read the Bible habitually: I need to set aside a daily quiet time. My time to read the Bible will be _____ .

    [ ] Tell God you're listening: It's time that I began my quiet time with a prayer to tell God I am listening to him.

    [ ] Ask God to show you how the Bible applies to your life: I am going to begin to prayerfully ask the Holy Spirit to apply his Word to my life. I am choosing to be more aware of how often God will speak Scripture to my heart about a situation.

    [ ] Wrestle with Scriptures you're not comfortable with: Instead of ignoring difficult and uncomfortable passages, I will welcome them into my life. In fact, I'm looking forward to the next difficult passage because I know it is an opportunity to experience amazing breakthrough's with God.

    [ ] Listen often to Godly teachers: Take a moment to write down the names of some teachers or preachers you think will help you as you listen to them. You might run their names by some people you respect, just to make sure their theology is sound.

    [ ] Engage with others: Write the names of some people you consider your spiritual mentors. People you can discuss what you are reading in God's Word and how you interpret it. Be sure to tell them that you see them in this role in your life.

    [ ] Predecide: If you've been reading and then deciding if you will obey or not, you might find a great personal break through if you tell God ahead of time that whatever he tells you to do, you'll do it.

    If you can, take a moment to honestly pray this prayer:

    Lord, whatever you want, whatever you reveal to me, I choose today to obey you.

8 Break New Ground With Your Emotions

> *Elijah was a man just like us. He prayed earnestly that it would not rain, and it did not rain on the land for three and a half years. Again he prayed, and the heavens gave rain, and the earth produced its crops.*
>
> James 5:17-18

I identify deeply with Elijah. The guy really blesses my soul. Know why? Because he was a complainer. His apprentice, the man who would later carry his mantel, was a man named Elisha. He did everything with amazing joy. He's harder for me to really connect with. But Elijah and I could have been buddies.

Truth #5
The Lord deeply cares about your personal suffering

As previously stated, the appearance of Moses and Elijah at the Transfiguration represents the Law and the Prophets. Both the Law and the Prophets predicted a Messiah would come. In their respective roles, they give testimony that Jesus is the fulfillment of the Scriptures.

At the Transfiguration, something very personal happened to each of these men. In this chapter, we'll study what God did in Elijah's life and how it culminated at the Transfiguration.

Elijah was a man of great intensity. He knew and experienced God deeply. He also hit a spiritual low point. Emotionally he was empty. He became so discouraged he asked God to let him die. Godly people who had walked with God, people who have previously broken through barriers spiritually, can still encounter spiritual drought. Godly people can encounter serious emotional pain. If you've ever been there, Elijah is your man too.

Break New Ground With God

When I turned sixteen, my grandpa gave me my first car. Actually, he gave me his car. It was a 1979 Chrysler LeBaron. Apparently 1979 was the Chrysler experiment year; everything had to be special ordered. Sometimes the car wouldn't start. You'd have to *prime it* to get it going. We took it on a family trip once; but it caught fire. That car also ate oil. It didn't leak oil, it just ate it. I'd be driving along, and suddenly the oil light would come on. I had to carry oil in the trunk of the car.

My dad told me, "Son, as soon as the oil light comes on, you have to pull over. Because if you run out of oil, you aren't going any further."

Some of you might be out of oil. You're tired. Spiritually drained. Physically exhausted. And yet, life demands you keep going. But the truth is, the walk with God that used to give you great strength and joy, is now in a state of drought.

What we see in Elijah is a man out of oil. When Elijah was at his worst, God did not give up on him. Even though there was a terrible valley, Elijah finished well. His appearance at the Transfiguration is a sign of the victory God gave him over his own brokenness.

The Bad Ole Days

After King Solomon, Israel went through a civil war that divided the nation into two parts. Israel had 19 wicked kings—in a row. Over and over, the Bible tells us that these *kings did evil in the eyes of Yahweh*. Each time it seemed things couldn't get worse, an even worse king would take over.

Things hit rock bottom when King Ahab took the throne. His father, Omri, had been a successful man in the eyes of the world, but failed to lead his family, or nation, to follow God. One of Omri's worst mistakes was sealing a political alliance with the marriage of his son, Ahab, to a lady named Jezebel.

Jezebel introduced her husband to the worship of Baal, and together they led the nation to seek Baal's blessing. The people were taught that Baal was a god of rain and fertility. He controlled the seasons and the crops. First Kings 16:33 says that Ahab did more than any other King to provoke Yahweh's anger.

As Israel turned from God, Elijah stepped onto the scene. Elijah's name means, *My God is Yahweh*. Elijah declared that because the people had rejected the true God and chosen to put their hope in

Baal, the Lord would withhold rain from the land. There wouldn't even be dew on the ground. Elijah was like the Martin Luther of his day, boldly declaring to those in power, "Here I stand! I can do nothing else."

God was good on his word. The sky shut up like bronze and there was no rain. If we read only the account in 1 Kings, we are left with the impression that Elijah stood alone on the stage of history and called for the drought. But he had a secret: James 5:17-18 states that Elijah prayed *earnestly* that it would not rain. Did you catch that? Like Jesus, his strength was his prayer life. He stood confidently in public because behind the scenes he was praying his heart out.

God does everything with a purpose. The purpose of the drought was not just to punish the nation, but to cause desperation. The drought would force people to reconsider what they really believed. Was Baal really a god? As thirst came and crops died, the nation's drought would become a symbol of their spiritual condition. God is willing to bring temporary discomfort and pain in order to spur repentance.

God Provided for Elijah

As the drought ravaged Israel, God took care of Elijah. He sent him to the Kerith Ravine east of the Jordan, where he could drink from the brook. Even more amazing was that ravens brought him bread and meat each morning and evening. That's amazing, first because birds don't usually feed people, people usually feed birds. But also, ravens by nature don't give up their food. They're like teenage boys, always hungry—ravenous. To care for Elijah, God changed the nature of the bird.

When the brook dried up, God sent Elijah to the town of Zarephath in Sidon where he found a widow gathering sticks. Because she honored God's prophet and had faith, God caused her supply of flour and oil to not run out. God didn't send Elijah to the Bible belt—he sent him to the heart of Baal worship. God sent him to a woman who was a Gentile unbeliever. Worse, her god was probably Baal, Elijah's arch enemy. Elijah thinks he's supposed to be fighting Baal worshipers, and in the middle of a great drought, God sends Elijah to Baal land to bless Baal worshipers. God is making it very clear to Elijah: I love people who are very lost. People who worship the wrong thing.

Break New Ground With God

Sometimes Christians act as if being a disciple of Jesus means we don't have to love certain people. Hollywood, gays, homeless, Muslims: the list can go on and on. But God is teaching Elijah, and us with him, that he wants us to have a heart as big as his. Bluntly, God loves sinful people. God wants us to remember that he's at war with Satan, but he loves people.

During the years of the drought, God cared for Elijah in the most unexpected ways.

Elijah's Test on Mount Carmel

After three years of no rain, Elijah knew it was time to call the people of God back to the Lord. He proposed to King Ahab that they gather on Mount Carmel for a test. The altar on top of Mount Carmel was broken down; no one worshiped there anymore.

When everyone had gathered on the mountaintop, Elijah asked the people how long they would keep trying to serve two gods. Like so many today, the people of that day did not outright reject Yahweh, they just thought they could add Baal in the mix. Yahweh was a god, in their view, but he was just one of many. Elijah rejected that thinking. There is only room in the universe for one God.

The prophets of Baal went first. They danced, shouted, prophesied, and called on the name of Baal from morning till noon. Of course, Baal doesn't answer because Baal doesn't exist. Alfred Edersheim suggested that Baal worship would remind many of us of voodoo.

At noon, Elijah began to give the prophets a hard time. Where was Baal? Why wasn't he answering? Perhaps what they needed to do was shout louder. Or maybe, Elijah suggested, Baal is deep in thought. Maybe thinking is hard for Baal, like moving big rocks, and he has to concentrate. Or maybe, Elijah suggested, Baal is busy. That is a Hebrew euphemism for going to the bathroom. I mean, it makes sense that Baal might need to relieve himself, after all, they feed him, right? Elijah even offered the idea that maybe Baal was traveling. Maybe he's just late. Get Elijah's taunts? Maybe Baal is not strong; maybe he's not smart; maybe he's so earthly that he has to use the restroom; maybe he's not fast.

In desperation, the prophets of Baal began to slash themselves with their spears. The Bible notes that this was their *custom*. Their religious practices led them to mutilate their own bodies. The re-

Chapter 8—Breaking New Ground With Your Emotions

sponse was silence. Baal did not answer. First Kings 18:29 says that no one paid attention.

When it was Elijah's turn, he repaired the altar with twelve stones representing the twelve tribes of Israel. He was there to call the nation home. When Joshua passed through the Jordan to take the Promised Land, he stacked twelve stones as a reminder. Now Elijah wants to remind them of the powerful God who brought them into the land.

Elijah put a sacrifice on the altar and had water poured on the altar three times. This was just to prove that a true miracle was about to take place. Elijah prayed a simple prayer, asking God to bring his people back.

God answered Elijah with fire. It is interesting that 1 Kings 18:38 says that *fire fell*. But look closely at the verse. It does not say that fire fell from Heaven, it says the fire of God came down. *"Then the fire of Yahweh fell..."* Not fire *from* Yahweh, the fire *of* Yahweh.

Does that remind you of Mount Sinai, where God came down on the mountain in fire? Maybe God himself came down on Mount Carmel that day in fire. Hebrews 12:29 states that God is a *consuming fire*. He appeared to Moses in a burning bush and led the people with a pillar of fire.

The people's reaction is classic! All through the account, the people have been acting like, "We don't know the answer. We don't know who is God." Then, after fire has fallen from Heaven, the altar is burning, they can hear the fire cackling as the wood burns, they can feel the warmth and they say, "Yahweh, he is God." Think Elijah wanted to go, "Do you think?!"

It was a day of great victory for Elijah. He ordered the prophets of Baal to be seized. They marched the false prophets to the brook of Kishon and executed them there.

As God's people turned back to him, Elijah turned himself to prayer and asked God to send rain. From one tiny cloud, the sky soon became black and rain began to pour. As the rain came, King Ahab was rushing home in his chariot. He was anxious to get in from the rain and to report to his wicked wife Jezebel all that had happened. Then, *the power of the Lord came upon Elijah and, ... he ran ahead of Ahab all the way to Jezreel.*

In that moment, Elijah must have felt incredible. He'd seen the fire of God; he'd been witness to the execution of the wicked prophets of Baal; and then he began to run like he'd never ran before. No one had ever seen someone run like Elijah ran that day. The rain smacked his face; something Elijah had not felt in three years.

He felt good.

And then it all fell apart.

When it all Dries Up

As long as the drought burned around him, Elijah stayed spiritually strong. His walk with God was powerful. He even raised a dead boy during the drought. But on the heels of the great victory, Elijah hit a brick wall spiritually.

Have you ever had this happen? You made it through the storm, but then for reasons that made no sense, you felt life collapse around you. Worse, your walk with God suddenly felt hollow. We often run to the story of Mount Carmel, which is awesome—but we must not miss what happened next, because it applies to all of us.

When King Ahab got back to his palace, he told his wife Jezebel what had happened. She burst into a rage and sent Elijah a message: You killed my prophets—I'm going to kill you. In a History Channel documentary on Jezebel, a commentator said that she was just misunderstood. Amazing modern liberal theology tries to make the bad guys the good guys. There's no misunderstanding Jezebel's message—I'm going to kill you.

You'd think Elijah would have some saucy answer like he'd had up on the mountaintop when confronting the prophets of Baal. But he had no come back.

In fact, Elijah became very afraid. He'd run to the place in the power of the Holy Spirit, but now he turned and in his own strength began to run away. Not only was he afraid, but when he got to Beersheba he left his servant there and went into the desert alone. And there, afraid and alone in the desert, dark thoughts began to overtake him.

Elijah made a request of God. Earlier he had prayed that the nation might come back and that God might show them that he was a true prophet of the true God. But now, his prayer is very different. "I've had enough, God," he prayed. "Let me die, I'm not better than all those who came before me."

Chapter 8—Breaking New Ground With Your Emotions

Exhausted, Elijah then lay down under a broom tree and slipped into a deep sleep.

We are often vulnerable to Satan's attack after great spiritual victories or milestones. It was after his baptism that Satan tempted Jesus to give up on his mission. It was after the storm and flood that Noah got drunk. It was after a series of great battles that David looked lustfully at a woman and fell into adultery.

We Often get Tired

A while back I went to a local book store and discovered a little treasure; a 1938 copy of *The Grapes of Wrath*. My mother-in-law Dee Dee once asked my daughter Annie if she knew what the Great Depression was. "Yes," Annie said, "It's the day before school."

I was very happy to find the copy of *The Grapes of Wrath*. The old bookstore proprietor ran his hands wistfully over the book.

"Ah, this is a good one. This would be worth a lot if it had its original book cover." Looking up at me he asked, "May I quote you a line?"

"Sure."

"As the Joads come into California, the old granny says, 'I'm tiiiired, and restin' don't do me no good.' "

Do you ever feel that way? Tired, and resting doesn't seem to do any good. Because it's not just your body that is weary, it's your soul.

Finally, Elijah got up and traveled forty days and forty nights until he reached Mount Horeb. Remember that name? It's also called Mount Sinai. It's where God gave Moses the law. It's also where the people asked God not to speak to them. Elijah felt so empty, he was hoping to hear from God. He went back to the place where God had made a covenant with his people and climbed up the sacred mountain.

God did appear to Elijah in a mighty way, and he asked Elijah what was wrong. Elijah explained it to the Lord this way, "I've been very zealous for you, Lord. But faithfulness isn't working so well. Your people have rejected the covenant and turned their back on you. They've killed all your prophets, torn down all your churches and it turns out, I'm the only one left. But bad news on that, God, they're trying to kill me too."

Elijah feels so discouraged because it seems like things are never going to change. Even if God sent fire on a mountaintop, Jezebel would not turn her heart to God. Even when God did move, it didn't seem like God did enough to really change the situation. Now, we can stand back and say, "Wait a minute, Elijah! All the prophets of Baal were killed! The people repented! Don't let Jezebel get you down." But in his exhaustion and pain, the threat from Jezebel consumed him and fueled the darkness.

We can get discouraged when we think the situation is never going to change. Nehemiah must have felt like he would never get the wall built. Job felt like he'd never get well. Abraham and Sarah thought they'd never have a child. Naomi, Ruth's mother-in-law, thought life could never be sweet again. And Elijah thought things could never get better. No matter how much he worked, no matter how big the miracles were, they just didn't seem like it was enough to make a difference. He was trying to empty the ocean with a thimble.

Sometimes after a long period of deeply serving God, even seeing success, we experience temptation, depression, and hit a spiritual wall. Even though we've been doing a lot and even growing, suddenly it seems like we haven't really accomplished much. "Things haven't really changed," the enemy whispers in our ear.

Haunting Amusement Parks

A few years ago, my daughter Annie and I watched a video about broken down amusement parks. It was haunting. Desolate Ferris Wheels; roller coasters overgrown with weeds, vines and even trees. The video spent quite a bit of time showing footage from Six Flags New Orleans, which was destroyed by hurricane Katrina. Six Flags chose not to rebuild the park, and it lies in ruins. Massive steel coasters rusted with time, and towers now limp. Huge rides are in disrepair and the wood structures that once served as ride stations are coming apart.

What's so haunting about those scenes? A theme park is supposed to be a place where there is life, laughter, screaming, and voices mingled together. Instead, there is just ominous silence and decay.

For some people, that describes their spiritual life. It was once full of joy, laughter and life. They couldn't wait to get into God's Word. But now their Bible is covered in dust, hardly read and their prayer life is broken down.

Chapter 8—Breaking New Ground With Your Emotions

If that's you, would you take a moment and pray, "Lord, I want to come back. Rebuild my walk with you. Refresh my spirit. Return to me the joy of my salvation."

How God Ministers to a Hurting Servant

What does God do when I hurt? First Kings 19 records several things that God did to restore Elijah. Even though Elijah was at the bottom emotionally, physically, and spiritually—God still loved him deeply. Elijah's feelings did not change God's reality.

1. God cared for Elijah's physical needs. After Elijah lay down under the broom tree, an angel from God came down and touched him. Pause there. The angel didn't have to touch him. Elijah probably needed to be touched. In fact, this would happen twice, and both times the angel came to him, he touched him. God knew Elijah's most basic needs. We would probably never say, "I just need to feel another person. I just need to be touched." But God knew.

God also knew that Elijah needed food. After the angel woke him, he told Elijah to get up and eat. Elijah must have been surprised to see warm bread and a jar of water sitting there. Jesus once told us that our Heavenly Father knows what we need before we ask (see Matthew 6:8).

God also knew that Elijah needed rest. After eating, Elijah again curled up under the broom tree and slept some more—until the angel came a second time. After eating and drinking, he was able to make the long journey to Mount Sinai (see 1 Kings 19:8).

God cares about your most basic physical needs. He knows you need to rest, that's why he commanded we take the Sabbath day and resist the urge to just keep working. When we give our employer an honest work week, and then take time to rest, we are giving honor to God. In essence, by taking time to rest, we are telling the lost world, "I've got a great God who allows me to rest." When we don't ever rest, we are communicating something very negative about God. We are saying to those around us, "My god is a slave driver—he doesn't give me any rest at all." The truth is, God invites us to not only work, but spend a day enjoying the fruit of our labor.

When we choose not to rest, we do damage to our spiritual life. When you don't rest, you become more susceptible to depression. You are more likely to lash out at people you love as your emotions are on edge. Weariness makes problems seem bigger than they really are. When we are tired, even serving God is no longer a joy but a chore.

If you've been stuck spiritually, and there is not a specific sin you need to repent of, I would suggest you examine your schedule. It's important to be serving God, working hard in your profession and caring for the needs of your family. But maybe in the grind of life, you forgot to take care of yourself physically. Maybe you need to re-examine your diet or make the decision to take a day to rest and enjoy your family.

2. God listened to Elijah's broken spirit. After Elijah had gone to Mount Sinai, he climbed into a dark cave in the mountain. If he felt alone in the desert, he must have felt very alone in that mountain cave. Yet, God found Elijah in the darkness and asked Elijah what he was doing there. In other words, God had not told Elijah to go into the desert alone or to make a journey to Mount Sinai. Elijah's ministry is to the lost and hurting people of Israel—not to mountain goats on Sinai.

When God asked Elijah what he was doing in the cave, Elijah just burst. And God didn't interrupt him. He let Elijah whine it out. To us, Elijah's prayer can sound proud and arrogant. He is telling God that he's given him all and he's the only faithful person left in Israel (see 1 Kings 19:10). Of course that ridiculous! But it's how he felt. And the truth is, you've probably felt that way sometimes, too. Ever feel like you're the only one serving at church? How come you're the only one willing to show up on work day? What would they do if you just decided to up and quit? Why, they'd be up the creek without a paddle—because you're the only one!

Well, it might sound crazy in the harsh black and white this book is written in, but in the colors of our emotions, we do feel that way sometimes.

Most of us are pretty toxic with our hurt. We complain everywhere. We sulk to ourselves and our anger leaks out in little comments that leave others wondering, "What's wrong with him?" Too often we take our hurts to our friends, or hairstylist, or social media.

Chapter 8—Breaking New Ground With Your Emotions

With Elijah, God showed us something important. As we listen to God, God also listens to us. He allows us to cry it out. In Psalm 142 David announced that he also was a complainer. Do you know who he complained to? God!

I cry aloud to the LORD;
I lift up my voice to the LORD for mercy.
I pour out my complaint before him;
before him I tell my trouble.

— Psalm 142:1-2

If prayer was the secret to Jesus' strength, it was the secret of Elijah's healing. He was able to take his hurts to God. And God listened to him.

3. God slowed Elijah's need for dramatics. After letting Elijah spill out his heart, God told him to step outside because Yahweh was about to physically pass by. Remember, this is the same mountain where Moses asked to see the glory of God, but God would only allow him to see his back (see Exodus 33:18).

Elijah went outside, and a great wind ripped through the mountains. Rocks fell as if bowing before Yahweh. But, the text notes that Yahweh himself was not in the wind. Where was God? He had promised to show up. After the wind, there was an earthquake, and once again God was not in the earthquake. Then there was a fire. Elijah knew all about fire! He had been there when the presence of God had fallen on Mount Carmel in fire! Certainly he had read Moses account of how God came down in fire on this same mountain. But, God was not in the fire. Finally, the Bible says there was a *thin silence*. What does that mean? The NIV calls it a *gentle whisper*. Sounds almost like someone breathing quietly.

In the quiet, Elijah would find God.

Elijah was a man of great theatrics. He was known for bold prophecies, commanding rain to stop, or fire to come from Heaven. At that moment, God knew that Elijah didn't need more noise. You can almost hear God whispering Psalm 46:10 to his heart—Elijah *be still and know that I am God.*

We can get so busy looking for the next big thing, that we miss God. More than likely, Elijah wanted not only fire on the mountain and the death of the prophets, he wanted Jezebel to repent and the whole nation all at once come back to God in a gigantic revival. When God didn't do it that way, Elijah probably was very disappointed.

Sometimes God uses small things. God uses small churches, and small children, and small steps forward to accomplish his purposes.

We want to break new ground with God all at once. We want to break new ground with God with a lot of noise. We want it to come in a big rush. But God often asks us to just stay faithful, and he will get us there one step at a time. We don't have to restore the whole nation at once, we just need to witness to our lost friend. We don't need to fill a stadium today for Jesus, we need to reach out to the lady next door who needs someone to help at her shop.

As a pastor, it worries me when people are always searching for the next big thing. They hop and bop from one church to another, looking for the best show in town. They want to experience God in all of God's bigness. But the real breakthrough will come when they decide to quiet their heart—be still and serve him day by day.

Do you know what Joshua's job was before he became Moses' successor and lead the nation to conquer the key cities of the Promised Land? He was called Moses' *aide*. His job was guarding the tent of meeting. There were exciting times at the tent of meeting. Times when God's glory would come down; the people would gather; Moses would enter the tent and come out with his face glowing. Joshua's job was to guard the tent and make sure no one entered it who wasn't authorized. But then, there were long periods of—nothing. Quiet. And when it was quiet, Joshua was still there. Everyone showed up when God came down and Moses' face glowed. But it was in the silence that Joshua served God the longest.

As much as God loves people who can do big things for him, We can too quickly overlook the importance of faithfulness in small things; reading the Bible daily, raising kids and having a family Bible time, and serving God as a Sunday School teacher both when the church is full and when attendance is down.

God can use small steps in your spiritual journey to get you further than the big ones will get you.

4. God reassured Elijah's heart. God told Elijah in 1 Kings 19:15 that he should go back the way he came, and there were some people God wanted him to anoint. One was the next king of Aram, and the other was Elijah's successor, a man named Elisha. Anointing kings and spiritual leaders is prophet's work. God was telling Elijah—

Chapter 8—Breaking New Ground With Your Emotions

I'm not done with you. You want to curl up and die, you feel like you haven't been a success, but you are still vital to my kingdom work.

It can't be emphasized enough how much 1 Kings 19 reflects Moses at Mount Sinai—the fire, the earthquake, the presence of God. Moses was in the wilderness forty years—Elijah made a forty day journey. God probably set this up to show Elijah that just as the Lord was with Moses, he was with Elijah. And just as Moses had a great role to play in God's kingdom, so did Elijah. It might seem looking back on it that Moses had a better assignment—after all, he got to lead the entire nation! Poor Elijah just didn't feel like he could make any headway. But to God, Elijah was a great success.

Sometimes we need to allow God to remind us that serving him is a big deal. Our work does matter. We are making an eternal impact, even when we can't see it. And those moments we are ready to give up, God says, "Hey, I still have work for you."

God didn't need Elijah looking for the next big thing—he just needed Elijah taking the next step forward.

5. God opened Elijah's eyes. God listened patiently to Elijah, then he showed his prophet what was really going on. Elijah was out of touch spiritually. He needed God's perspective. In fact, he needed correction. He was seeing things all wrong. God showed Elijah five things in 1 Kings 19:15-17.

First, God revealed to Elijah that he was not where he needed to be. He needed to get up and go back the way he came.

Second, God made it clear that he was still King of the nations. God ordered Elijah to go and anoint Hazael to be king of Aram and Jehu the king of Israel. God let Elijah know that he had a plan for the nations. God had not slipped off his mighty throne while Elijah struggled with a bout of depression. God was still God.

We get discouraged sometimes because we don't see God's plan. We just have to trust him, one step at a time and obey him, believing all the way that he sees the big picture and is using our steps of obedience. Elijah didn't need to move the nations—he just needed to respond to God obediently. It is amazing how a talk with God about the need to obey him can change our perspective, encourage our hearts, and repair a struggling faith.

Third, God made it clear that he, in his own time and way, would judge the ungodly. He explained to Elijah that Jehu, Hazael and Elisha would be agents of his judgment. So, while it may look to Elijah that wicked people like Jezebel just get away with their evil, the truth was that God would execute judgment in his time. Elijah didn't need to get depressed about the state of the world or how bad things were, God was very much at work all around him.

We sure do get impatient with God's timing, don't we? We want God to punish our enemies quickly. But remember what Peter said about the Lord's Coming? God is patient with us because he wants many to come to repentance. But he is moving the world according to his sovereign plan toward a day of final judgment.

Fourth, God showed Elijah that he was not alone. Elijah felt like the last man on earth serving God. But actually, God had already chosen Elijah's eventual replacement, Elisha, his associate. On Mount Sinai, God told Elijah to go anoint Elisha to be his successor. God was reminding him that his time on earth was limited, so he needed to focus on God's purposes. God needed Elijah to get down to the business of training Elisha and preparing the next generation for kingdom service. God was making it very clear to Elijah that he was not at all alone.

Fifth, God informed Elijah that he still has a remnant in Israel. Not only was Elijah not alone, God explained that he actually had seven thousand who had never worshiped Baal (see 1 Kings 19:18). Romans 11:2-6 speaks of this same verse. The Apostle Paul tells us that just as God reserved a small group of true believers in Israel during Elijah's day, so also in our day God has a group of believers in Israel who have not rejected God. There will always be a group of true believers, a remnant, in Israel.

While it is encouraging to know that God uses small people in big ways, sometimes our hearts need to be reminded that God has a lot of other people who serve him as well. Sometimes my wife and I leave the desert where I pastor and drive to Saddleback Church. It's huge! And somehow, it encourages my heart to stand in a room with four or five thousand other believers and worship God.

Putting Truth into Action

Much of what Elijah learned in his experience at the mountain with God was not new. I'm sure he already had been taught many years earlier that God was sovereign over the nations. Elijah also knew that God cared about him. But when he ran from Jezebel, he seems to have forgotten some things that God needed to remind him of.

Chapter 8—Breaking New Ground With Your Emotions

How could Elijah forget that God rules over the nations? Or, how could he doubt that God cared for him? On the mountain, he struggled emotionally with God's justice and provision. He felt alone, abandoned and overwhelmed. He might have learned long ago—even preached it himself—that God is king of the world; but at that moment as he spoke to God, he didn't feel it. In that cave, Elijah didn't learn new things about God, he reengaged with the truth he already knew. Elijah had to re-believe what he already knew to be true.

There are many things we learned long ago that over time we begin to doubt. We learn as children that God loves us, but then life happens—bills overwhelm us and people hurt us—and soon we lose sight of God's love. To get back to spiritual health, we have to make the conscience decision to re-believe some things that are true that we let go over time.

We need to remember that...
- God cares deeply about us.
- God listens when our heart is broken.
- God provides our most basic needs, physically and emotionally.
- God speaks truth when our perspective is skewed.
- God sees things we don't see.
- God is at work even when we can't see it.

How do you Break New Ground with your Emotions?

Does it feel like you are controlled by how you feel? Are you easily jolted out of joy by a simple criticism? All can be going good, when suddenly you remember a past sin and feel frustrated and worthless. Do you begin to think about how much better others have it and how little progress you have made in life? Like Elijah, do you begin to emotionally sink?

When your emotions are under God's control, it is much easier for the rest of you to become obedient to the Lord. Have you ever given God your emotions, or do you feel captive to them? "I'm just an angry person, that's all there is to it," you may have said. "I can't control how I think." But you can.

It's About who you Listen To

God's command on the Mount of Transfiguration was that we must listen to Jesus. Yet, there are so many voices that want to crowd out God's voice.

Maybe you're out of oil spiritually. In order to allow God to minister to you there must be a decision on your part to filter out the other voices and listen for God. You can't move forward, you can't minister to others or make headway in your own walk with God until you restore your spiritual health.

You may need to spend some time with God telling him exactly how you feel. Do you feel alone? Feel like no one understands you? Feel like you're the only one serving the Lord? Tell him that.

But then, ask God to show you his perspective. God's perspective and his voice are best found through his Word, the Bible.

When I was a teen, I decided I should teach my sister to drive: in my grandpa's backyard. So, there we were, in the 1979 Chrysler, doing circles in his big backyard. I felt so important. And she was doing so good. Doing good, that is, until she started toward the chain link fence that divided grandpa's property from the cranky neighbor.

"Hey, look out for the..."

I didn't finish. She went right into that fence and then kind of bounced off. Looking for the brake, she accidently hit the gas and floored it! We went right back into that chain link fence. The pole holding the fence just bowed right down like it was the second coming of Jesus. Finally, she found the brake: dust flowered up around us as we got out.

"Well," I said, looking between the kneeling fence and a car that looked like it was trying to catch its breath, "I don't think you dented the car a bit. But the fence..."

"Uh-oh," my sister said, pointing. "He looks mad."

Storming across the neighbor's yard—we could see him real good because the fence was out of the way—came my grandpa's grouchy neighbor. Oh, he let us have it!

"What are you kids doing?"

"I'm teaching my sister to drive."

"I know, I saw you! But she shouldn't be learning in a back yard. She should be out on the highway."

I stared numbly at the fence, unsure we should be on the highway.

Chapter 8—Breaking New Ground With Your Emotions

After chewing us out, the neighbor eventually ran out of words and went in. I parked the car and went in to report to grandpa what had happened. He'd already seen it.

"Took down the fence, eh?" grandpa said with a grin.

"Well, we just bent the pole a little," I said. "But the neighbor was really mad."

Grandpa's eyes lit up. "He was mad at you? Why?"

I shrugged, "You know, because of the fence and all."

"Why, he shouldn't say a word to you about it. It's my fence. I put it there. If Karyn wants to drive a car into my fence, what business is it of his?"

There we had been, listening to that guy chew us out over something that didn't even belong to him. It wasn't his fence. He didn't have any authority over us. He just wanted someone to rant at.

Often we let the devil in to rant at us. He tells us we're making a mess of things, or not getting good results, or that we are terrible failures.

In 1 Kings 19:15, God told Elijah to go back the way he came. And then he corrected all of Elijah's thinking. Elijah was just too busy listening to the wrong voices. He needed to get back to the business of letting God define him and his ministry and his nation.

We can break new ground with God when we choose to listen to his voice. When he is the one who comforts us, heals us and confronts us. Satan has a lot he'd like to say to us, but his words are venom, not healing. When God corrects us, there is great healing because in his correction is right direction.

Digging Deeper

1. Have you ever gone from a great spiritual victory to a deep emotional valley?

    [ ] Yes   [ ] No

2. Why do you think Elijah went back to Mount Sinai?

    _____
    _____
    _____

3. What part of Elijah's story do you most identify with?

    _____
    _____
    _____

4. What are some practical ways God has taken care of you in dark hours?

    _____
    _____

5. How obedient have you been to God's command to rest on the Sabbath and enjoy his goodness? Not as an act of legalism, but out of the overflow of a thankful heart.

    _____
    _____

    - What changes to your schedule will you need to make in order to take a day of rest?

        _____
        _____

Chapter 8—Breaking New Ground With Your Emotions

6. Have you ever allowed yourself to complain to God?

    [ ] Yes   [ ] No

    - Entire Psalms are dedicated to complaining. They are called a "lament." You might take some time to write down your complaint as a lament.

    _____
    _____
    _____

    - How do you think God responds to your complaints?

    _____
    _____
    _____

7. How do you separate your own misconceptions and wrong opinions from God's truth?

    _____
    _____
    _____

8. Are you easily taken in by a big show?

    [ ] Yes   [ ] No   [ ] Sometimes

    When was the last time you simply enjoyed God in the quiet?

    _____
    _____
    _____

9 What You Have To Drop To Finish Well

Behold, I am coming soon! My reward is with me, and I will give to everyone according to what he has done.
Revelation 22:12

Elijah's life is like a mountain road, rising and falling. Sometimes he hit the mountaintop, and other times his life wound down into the canyons of depression. But here's what's important about Elijah—he didn't quit.

> **Truth #6**
>
> **Faithfulness in the face of hardship will be greatly rewarded**

Elijah had an hour of deep discouragement, a point where he just wanted to die. But God wasn't playing that game. He had more for Elijah to do. He needed Elijah to get spiritually healthy so he could finish well.

Maybe, like Elijah, you've been out of oil spiritually. As God restores your soul, it's important to make the decision to not give up. Any of us who have served long in church know of people who just decided to quit. They didn't go to another church; they didn't even change religions. They just stopped with God. It was a thing they did; a season of life, but they didn't make it to the end.

God Rewarded Elijah Greatly

Elijah did not live an easy life. There were moments he wanted to give up. Because he stayed faithful in the darkest hours, God rewarded Elijah greatly. Elijah was one of only two people in the Bible who never died; the other is Enoch (see Genesis 5:21-24). Enoch seems to have walked to Heaven with God. Elijah's entrance to heaven was more dramatic. As he and his friend, Elisha, walked down the road, a chariot of fire broke through the boundary that stands between Heaven and earth and Elijah went up into Heaven through a whirlwind (see 2 Kings 2:11).

It's amazing how richly God rewarded Elijah's faithfulness. His experience was unparalleled. But God wasn't done rewarding Elijah.

Putting Truth into Action

Not only did Elijah not have to suffer the pain of physical death; long after he had ascended to Heaven, he was allowed to return to earth. This time he came with Moses to stand at the Transfiguration and discuss with the Messiah his redemptive work on the cross.

It seems obvious that God chose Moses to stand with Jesus at the Transfiguration because he was the author of the Torah—the Law. But why Elijah? Why not Isaiah or Jeremiah or one of the writing prophets? The short answer is—God's word doesn't say. A lot of people think they know, but ultimately it was God's choice. God chose to bring Elijah with him to the Mount of Transfiguration.

Elijah must have felt honored. He stood as a representative of the prophets, communicating with Jesus about the events soon to unfold in Jerusalem. Did he and Moses bring a word of encouragement? Surely, just their presence must have greatly encouraged Jesus.

Think about this: Just when Elijah thought it couldn't get any better, it got better. Why? Because God rewards faithfulness lavishly. When it comes to love and rewards, God's a liberal.

John Cleves Symmes was an officer in the war of 1812. After the war, he spent his life promoting the idea that the earth was hollow. While many scientific reasons for this idea were floated, Cleves and his followers also offered a theological reason for their theory. They suggested that God had created the earth hollow as means of *economy*. They argued that God would not waste matter. In their view, God was frugal. The problem is that it's not only scientifically wrong, it was wrong about God. God is in reality extravagant. Just look at how richly God rewarded Elijah.

God will generously and extravagantly reward those who are faithful. Living by faith is worth it.

Let's look a little deeper at what it means to faithfully live for Jesus so that we can be richly rewarded on the Final Day.

Run Hard and Finish the Race

Here's the secret to having more faith—faithfulness. Doesn't that sound dumb? Faith requires faithfulness.

Faithfulness = Greater Faith

Often, people who have a deep-rooted faith are people who have been at it for a long time. They have been through storms and on mountaintops: through it all they have held on to their faith. They've built spiritual muscle. They've built stamina and learned to endure.

The Bible compares living by faith to running a race. It takes focus, sacrifice, and determination to finish well.

In 1 Corinthians 9:24, the Apostle Paul reminded us that all the runners run in a race, but there's only one who gets the prize. Then he commanded us to:

Run in such a way as to get the prize.

— 1 Corinthians 9:24

He wants us to finish well.

Running is a simple visual sport. It's not like football, baseball, or basketball where you have to try to keep up with what's going on. My grandfather loved wrestling—Spanish wrestling. He didn't speak Spanish. Given that he was deaf, it wasn't hard for him to track what was happening. Paul chose a sport where there would be a clear, visual way to see who was ahead and who won.

In Acts 20:24, Paul says that he considers his life nothing, he just wants to finish the race. And then in a letter to Timothy, his beloved son in the ministry, Paul says...

I have fought a good fight, I have finished my course, I have kept the faith.

— 2 Timothy 4:7, KJV

Look at four words from that verse: *fought, fight, finished, kept.* They are all words to imply standing firm and fighting to the end. Paul was not ready to go out with a whimper; he was going to give Jesus Christ every last breath he had.

Over and over Paul is saying, "Don't drop out early!" The reason many don't have a strong faith is because they haven't stayed faithful. If you can't stay faithful to your marriage, how can your faith in God grow? The same is true in your ministry or your love for others. If

Break New Ground With God

you cannot continue to obey what God told you to do over a period of time, then your faith muscles are not strong enough to make a spiritual breakthrough.

We break new ground with God when we choose not to give up. It is so easy to get tired and discouraged, isn't it? We give something our best for a period of time, but after we don't see the results we want, the urge to quit can be overwhelming. There are spots in the race where we are tempted to fall along the side and say, "I just can't do it anymore." These might be times we need to rest and reconnect with God, but these are not times we need to throw in the towel.

If Paul was writing to us today he wouldn't use a foot race, he might use the example of a car race—NASCAR. The cool thing about racing cars is that most of us think, "I could do that." Because they're doing stuff we do all the time. It's disappointing for us to realize we probably can't do what they do.

Here's a sad truth: everyone won't win this race. Many will drop out along the way. Many will get exhausted and limp away. Some will not only quit, but return to the world. And a few will become hostile to Jesus, who they once served.

When it comes to faith, we should not want to trip, fall, or come up short. We should want to put the pedal to the metal. We should want to run (drive!) in a way that causes us to cross the finish line still going hard and fast.

We should want to finish like Elijah. The guy ran so hard, a whirlwind took him to Heaven!

Focus on Jesus

When the founder of the Salvation Army, William Booth, was on his deathbed, his attorney indicated there was a document he still needed to sign. They brought him the document and asked if he would be able to sign it. Yes, he said, he could and would sign the necessary paper. He signed and sealed the document. After he died, the document was opened and they discovered that instead of signing his own name on the paper, Booth had signed the name Jesus. As he prepared to move from this life to the next, Booth was so focused on Jesus that he forgot his own name.

The author of Hebrews writes:

Since we are surrounded by so great a cloud of witnesses, let us also lay aside every weight, and sin which clings so closely, and let us run with endurance the race that is set before us, looking to Jesus, the founder and perfecter of our faith, who for the joy that was set before him endured the cross, despising the shame, and is seated at the right hand of the throne of God.

— Hebrews 12:1-2, ESV

We are called to an amazing race. The author of Hebrews explains to us that if we intend to run well, we are going to have to strip down. Even today, runners in a race wear as little clothing as possible so that nothing hinders them.

If we want to really experience God like we never have before, according to the author of Hebrews, we must do two things—throw worry off our back and deal seriously with sin. The answer to both is in what we look at. If you look at the world, you will worry and sin. If you look at Jesus, he will never lead you to sin or cause you to worry.

Sounds great, right? Only thing is, most of us still focus on things we worry about and we still choose to indulge in sin. The result is a loss of focus on Jesus, and new ground is not broken. We just stay on the same hard ground.

Imagine what would happen if you actually chose to focus on Jesus. You would have a lot less stress. You would be very focused. You would be more productive because you would not be trying to fix problems you can't or wasting emotional energy on things that you can't change. More than that, focusing on Jesus would be cutting out some sins. You wouldn't be weighed down by old ways and guilt, but would have freedom to really live for Christ. You would break new ground with God. You would experience joy in your relationship with God like never before. Your coworkers would ask you why you have so much peace. What changed? Your family would notice how much more playful you are and happy to have them. You would no longer treat those around you like a burden, but would have the emotional energy to give to your relationships. All because you made the choice to actually stop worrying and give up stubborn sins.

Take Off the Weight of Worry

Just as Elijah went to the cave and poured his heart out to God, we will not be set free until we give God our worries and concerns.

Worry is spiritual pollution. It damages our connection to God, which is vital to knowing what God wants us to do. If we want a healthy prayer life, we must take our focus off the mess and put our focus on Jesus. But worry steals our focus from Jesus to the worldly way of handling trouble. We worry because we think God doesn't have something under control. We think God needs our help. Worry, like the weight that Hebrews describes, is simply a waste of energy. And when you're running a race, you don't want to waste any energy.

Jesus pointed out that birds don't waste their energy on worry, but God takes care of them. You don't see a raven pacing the branch, "What's the weather going to be tomorrow. Will there be any road kill?" You won't see a raven's nest with a storage nest attached! Birds don't worry, but we humans are really good at it. The result is—few people really break new ground with God because worry clogs up their walk.

After the Sunday service, when I preached on worry, a woman visiting the church for the first time, came up to me very upset. "Who told you I was coming today?" she demanded. She was upset because she was an habitual worrier, and was sure someone in her family found out she was coming to church and called me ahead of time to ask me to preach on worry.

"My friend," I told the woman, "we all struggle with worry."

And that's so sad, isn't it? Because it means that is an area that stops us from really enjoying God and the life he has for us.

Worry changes our personality. Have you ever worried so much that when you finally have a moment of peace, you wonder what you forgot? You're worried that you're not worried.

Worry is emotional atheism. It's anti-faith. It is the opposite of breaking new ground, worry hardens the ground. Just as failure to rest bears false witness against God, worry suggests that God will fail on his many promises. King David wrote:

I was young, now I'm old; in all my years:
　yet I have never seen the righteous forsaken.

— Psalm 37:25

Worry is dangerous because it chokes our walk with Jesus. Jesus said in Matthew 13:22 that the worries of this life can choke out the good seed of the Gospel. Some people, when they first hear the Gospel are very glad to hear of God's offer of mercy and grace. But they never really live for God, they don't even get started on the race, because their spiritual life gets stifled by exaggerated problems.

Chapter 9—What You Have To Drop To Finish Well

We can set aside our worries with two words—*Faithfulness* and *Focus*.

Our job is to be faithful to whatever God called us to do. Once God got Elijah to stop worrying, Elijah was able to focus on the Lord again and get back to the work of being a prophet. For us, it means staying faithful to the calling God has given us. To not get lazy in sermon preparation or church leadership. God's command for us not to worry is not an endorsement of spiritual laziness: it is a call for us to be faithful and trust him with the results.

If we are faithful to what God has told us to do, then the only other thing we need to do is focus our energy on Jesus. Don't get distracted by the problems around us: God is able to take care of us.

I pastor a church near a large military installation. It's encouraging to meet so many young people who have sacrificed greatly to serve our nation. Because so many people in our church are military, it means they are always moving. Ahead of one big transition, when we were about to lose a lot of people, I lay awake at night worrying over how we could rebuild the church. What if new people didn't come to replace all those leaving? Would the church wither and die?

In that night, in my Elijah cave, as I shared with God how worried I was. I deeply sensed God say something to me. It was very simple. "Stay faithful. I have not forgotten Palms Baptist." I was suddenly very awake. Why had God said that? Had I thought God had forgotten us? I certainly was acting like it.

The reformer Martin Luther once spent three days in a deep depression. When he finally came down stairs, his wife Katherine was dressed completely in black. He assumed she was mourning over someone's death.

"Who died?" Luther asked.

"God," his wife replied.

"God died? What do you mean? God cannot die."

"Well, the way you've been acting I was sure he had."

Stunned, Luther realized his wife was right. He etched in his desk the Latin word, *vivit*. It means *He lives*.

Throw Off the Weight of Sin: The Woman Caught in Adultery

In making Jesus our focus, Hebrews tells us not only to throw our worries overboard, but our sins as well.

Break New Ground With God

In John 8 we are confronted with a startling command from Jesus that mirrors Hebrews' command to throw off the sin that *so easily entangles* (Hebrews 12:1).

The Bible tells us that while Jesus was at the temple, the Scribes and Pharisees brought a woman who had been caught in the act of adultery and put her in front of Jesus. The Scribes were like the lawyers of their day, they were experts in the law. *"Moses commanded us to stone a woman caught in adultery,"* they said. *"But you, what do you say?"*

The question itself suggested Jesus might have an answer different than the Bible. Was his teaching outside the boundaries of Scripture? They were hoping so. Jesus bent down and wrote in the sand. No one knows what he was writing. The most popular view was that he was writing a list of her accusers' sins. Or maybe their names. Many people think he was writing a Scripture like Jeremiah 17:13 or Deuteronomy 9:10. It could even have been that Jesus was writing the Ten Commandments with his finger, as they were originally written in stone by the finger of God.

Finally, as they pressed Jesus to give an answer, Jesus said that those who were not guilty of sin could throw a stone at the woman.

What? He said they could stone her? No one expected him to uphold the law. They thought he would void it. But instead, brilliantly, he both upheld the law and made it painfully personal. That's what Jesus does when you listen to him. He brings the fire of God's Word so close it burns you.

Then Jesus bent down and went back to writing in the sand. I'm seriously curious what he was writing, since it brackets his statement. Maybe it was just, "Jesus was here." I know when I get to Heaven, I'm checking out the DVD. As Jesus wrote in the sand, those who had brought the woman to him began to leave, oldest to youngest.

One by one everyone left except Jesus. He didn't need to leave, because he hadn't committed any sin. He alone did have a right to judge her. Jesus asked her, *"Where are your accusers?"*

She must have been absolutely stunned. *"They're gone."*

Then Jesus said to her:

Neither do I condemn you; go, and from now on sin no more.

— John 8:11, ESV

Chapter 9—What You Have To Drop To Finish Well

What did he say? *Go and sin no more*!

All was going good when he said she could go. Go and live her life. Go and don't be condemned. Go and enjoy friends and family. Go and be happy no one threw stones at you today. But look at what he says next—*Go and sin no more*. Reflect on that. That's a harder command than don't worry.

Sure, Jesus, I'll just stop that sin thing now. I was getting tired of it anyway.

How can Jesus tell people to *sin no more*? You almost expect someone, maybe Peter, to pull Jesus aside and explain to him that this is a problem. "Look, you can't be telling people they can't sin. We know you don't sin. You never look twice at a girl. But we're kind of addicted to the sin thing. You can't go around telling people they can't sin."

Jesus' command to *sin no more* seems utterly impossible to obey. We have to sin, right? We're born in sin. Sin is powerful. We become defined by our sins. He's a drunk; she's a gossip; he's a womanizer; oh wow, does she ever have an anger problem; he's greedy; she's mean.

Jesus' command also seems impossible to keep because we think we cannot break loose from sin. Not only do we become defined by our sins, we become captives or slaves to sin. We think, "Jesus, please, please, please do not say *sin no more*. Because I'm chained to this stuff. I'm chained to my anger. I'm chained to my lust. It's become part of who I am."

But Jesus is not impressed or intimidated by sin's power. He simply urges her to *sin no more*.

But how are we supposed to just walk away from sin? I mean, face it, talk about breaking new ground with God! If we could get a handle on sin, then we could really move forward with the Lord. Things would change radically if we could just choose not to sin.

I was so interested in the verse that I wrote myself a note, "Study that text, and ask the question: How could she go and sin no more? He demanded she have victory over sin. Jesus would not have sent her with the command to *sin no more* if he did not give her the tools to *sin no more*. What did he do that allowed her to *sin no more*?"

Before Jesus told her to give up sin, he told her that he did not condemn her (see John 8:11). First, he removed her condemnation. He had mercy on her. Then he said, "*Sin no more*." The order of that is very important. First he set her free, and then he asked her to live in that freedom. Why be set free only to return to the old chains?

Jesus' mercy changed everything. Certainly Jesus' mercy changed her past. She was released from the guilt of adultery. He stopped them from stoning her and had mercy on her. He released her from her guilt. For us, God's mercy means that we do not have to suffer wrath for eternity in hell.

That's where most of us stop. With what mercy does for our past, God's mercy also set her future free as well. Mercy did more than affect her past or release her from punishment on judgment day; Jesus' mercy empowered her for what was to come. Jesus' mercy broke sin's grip on her future.

Jesus not only told her to *sin no more*, by having mercy on her, Jesus gave her the ability to *sin no more*.

Mercy Gives Us the Ability to Leave a Life of Sin

God's mercy opens the door to incredible spiritual freedom. We are given the very real opportunity to choose to walk away from sinful behavior. It is no longer just an act of our will. When we just try to be strong enough and break sinful habits, we often find we are terribly weak. But God's mercy not only wipes the slate clean, mercy gives us tools to live in radical victory over sin.

Often God's children act as if we are captives to sin; we think we can't escape. The truth is, as God's children, we are set free by his mercy. We can walk away from sinful behavior. There are some specific ways mercy frees us to walk away from sin and fully live for God.

God's mercy makes room for the Holy Spirit. When God forgives us of our sins, the Holy Spirit moves into our lives. It is the Holy Spirit who empowers us to live in a way that is holy and pleasing to God.

We hear Christians all the time say that they want the POWER of the Holy Spirit. They want the *power* to speak in tongues. They want the *power* to do miracles.

How about the power to stop cussing? Because you have it.

Guys tells me, "I just can't stop looking at porn." Yes you can. Don't tell me you are filled with the power that created the universe, but you can't stop looking at naked girls! Don't think that you are filled with the power that raised Lazarus from the dead, but you can't stop the affair. Don't believe for a moment that you are filled with the power that could calm a storm, but that same power can't help you to stop worrying.

Look at it in terms of the Transfiguration: do you think that Jesus could be glorified by God; shine with physical glory of God; have God declare from a cloud that he is God's Son; but somehow be weaker than your personal sin? If Jesus could conquer the grave, then he can give us the power to defeat perpetual sin. We have to *want* to.

Moses and Elijah were talking to Jesus about his exodus. In that exodus, he would set us free. He would, in his mercy, pass over our sins and offer himself as a substitute. But more than just forgive us of our sins, Jesus is ready to do what Moses could not. Take us into the Promised Land.

God's mercy shuts the enemy down. As long as we are in a state of perpetual sin, we are in Satan's clutches. But when we accept that God is good on his word, that he has really forgiven us, we are free from Satan's accusation. His power is broken and we have freedom to serve God with joy. In Romans 12:1, Paul urges us *in view of God's mercy, to offer your bodies as living sacrifices*. Because God had mercy on our past, we am free in the future to serve God.

In 2011, a couple of Florida homeowners, Warren Nyerges and Maureen Collier, were stunned when they got a foreclosure notice from Bank of America. In 2009, they paid for their house in cash. They never owed Bank of America a dime. But that didn't stop the bank from trying to collect. In fact, nothing could dissuade Bank of America. Finally, the couple went to court and proved before a judge that they didn't owe the bank any money. The judge agreed, and ordered the bank to pay their court expenses. When the bank refused to reimburse the couple, Nyerges and Collier did something amazing. They showed up with police at their local branch and effectively foreclosed on the bank. Police entered the branch bank and explained that if they did not issue a check for the court ordered amount, the police would begin to seize bank property. They would take computers, desks, and even cash drawers.

They foreclosed on the bank! God has already foreclosed on Satan. We should not give him the victory of stressing us about old sins already forgiven.

God's mercy also creates a sweet place to stay. Once we are at peace with God and not under the Spirits conviction, why would we want to go back to our old sins? Our walk with God will eventually decrease our desire to sin.

Break New Ground with God

To give up the self-destructive habits of sin and worry, the author of Hebrews urges us to focus on Jesus. That decision will require we give up some things we love in the flesh. It will force us to surrender our worries to God and let go of sins we really enjoy. Sin is fun for a season, but then it becomes painful.

Here's where we find new ground with God. We can walk away from the things we think we're trapped in. We can let go of worry: we are not prisoners of our minds; we are no longer slaves to sin. The great liberator of our souls died on the cross to set us free.

Here's an awkward question: what's your sin? To what do you need to say, "This is over. I'm done," in order for you to break new ground with God.

Hebrews tells us that our sins and our worries hold us down. But Jesus can set us free. The real question is this: do you *want* to be free? Are you happy living in sin? Are you okay with the weight of worry? If you continue sinning, you will not break new ground with God. But as soon as you say, "This is over. I repent of this sin and choose to follow Jesus," new ground is broken.

Living an Even Better Life

We can finish well if we get serious about worry and sin. We can be sure that God will abundantly reward those who sacrifice their wants and desires to follow him. Heaven is going to be great.

Elijah did not give up in the dark hours of his life. He pushed through, and ultimately found new ground in his walk with God. You would think the zenith of one's walk would be to stand on Mount Carmel and see fire fall from Heaven; but God had so much more in store for Elijah. There is so much Elijah would have missed if he had dropped out early. If he had allowed his depression, his sins, and his worries to consume him, he would have never rode the whirlwind to Heaven.

Elijah went from a broom tree where he wanted to just end his life, to a cave where he poured out his broken heart to God. But the story doesn't end there. Because he stayed faithful in his darkest days, God would give him the opportunity to train the great prophet

Chapter 9—What You Have To Drop To Finish Well

Elisha. And, God would sweep him into Heaven without the normal protocol of death.

The Transfiguration suggests something about Heaven that is very important—Heaven will have many new experiences.

Sometimes when I hear people talk about Heaven, they see it as kind of a flat line. That is, once you're there and checked out the place, there isn't much more to experience. What else is there to do but just keep eating more food? Thus, discussions about heaven often become strangely focused on what we plan to eat. Heaven is seen as an endless buffet instead of a place of incredible purpose. But both Moses and Elijah had new experiences ahead. The same will be true for us. We won't be taken down to a mountain to talk to the Messiah, but we will be offered new opportunities and new ways to serve God.

Heaven is not a Borg-like experience where you just become part of the collective. You continue to have a unique personality, memory and experiences. In other words, life goes on. Jesus calls it, eternal life. And in Jesus' teaching, eternal life does not start in Heaven, it starts with a relationship with him. Our true life, our eternal life, starts when we repent of sin and discover God's grace. That is our new life. And that new life here on earth keeps getting better as we come to know Jesus more and more. And then there is the great day of transformation—the day of our death. As the body dies and is eventually planted in the ground to await the resurrection, our spirit goes to the Lord to continue the next part of our eternal life.

Every day of eternity will be better than the one before it. There is nothing boring about God or Heaven. You might be tempted to quit now, to drop out early—but serving God is so worth it.

God has rewards you haven't even thought of. All we can think is, *big house* and *gold streets*!

Moses and Elijah never thought God would say to them one day, "Hey guys, let's go down to earth and talk to Jesus." That certainly must have totally excited them.

Know this, the God of Moses and Elijah is our God, too. If he richly rewarded them for their faithfulness, he's going to richly reward our faithfulness as well.

Digging Deeper

1. List some ways God rewarded people in the Bible.
   _____
   _____

2. Take time to reflect on how God has already rewarded you.
   _____
   _____

3. What are some specific things you are tempted to worry about?
   _____
   _____

4. Reflect honestly: have you been tricked into thinking there are some sin patterns you cannot break out of?

   [ ] Yes   [ ] No

5. Do you want to be free from sin and worry, or are you busy enjoying them?

   [ ] Want to be free   [ ] Do enjoy some

6. What will you do to focus on Jesus instead of worry and sin?
   _____
   _____
   _____

7. What are some things you are looking forward to about heaven?
   _____
   _____

10 Building On New Ground

> *Do not conform any longer to the pattern of this world, but be transformed by the renewing of your mind. Then you will be able to test and approve what God's will is—his good, pleasing and perfect will.*
> Romans 12:2

It's not enough to get to new ground—you need to build on it. Disciplines such as prayer, faith, Scripture reading, learning to trust God, and resisting sin are all very important. But eventually, we must carry these truths down the mountain and into the real world. They must impact not only how we think but how we live.

Coming down from the mountain must have been difficult for the disciples. We know they were chatty! The Bible tells us nothing about their conversation on the way up the mountain, but as they come down they are very engaged with Jesus about what's to come and what just happened.

After you break new ground with God, you can expect some things will happen. The next events and how you respond to them will determine if you have really broken new ground with God, or if you have just stuffed the building plans in your head and failed to actually build.

Expect—The Devil is Going to Be in Your Face

Soon after you begin making headway with God, you can expect some opposition from the enemy. Satanic forces are real and they are in our world coming in direct resistance to people of faith.

In Mark 9, after the Transfiguration, Jesus had a confrontation with a demon that is very memorable. Jesus and the three disciples came down from the mountain and found that the rest of the disciples had gotten very popular. Well, I don't know they were popular, but there was a crowd gathered around them. An argument was in full swing. But as soon as people spotted Jesus, they forgot their argument and came running to him. Of course, Jesus wanted to know what they were arguing about. A man in the crowd filled explained to Jesus that he had brought his son to the disciples. The boy was constantly under demonic attack, but the disciples couldn't heal him.

Jesus ordered that the boy be brought to him. When the boy was brought to Jesus, the demon went crazy. It did not want to be in the presence of Christ! As you study the Scriptures, note the great fear that demons have toward Jesus. He might have a human body, but they are well aware this is no ordinary man.

As the boy foamed at the mouth and rolled around, Jesus asked the father, *"how long has this been going on?"*

The man answered, *"Since he was a child. The demon often tries to hurt him, throwing him into fire or water. If you can do anything, please help us!"*

That statement startled Jesus.

"If you can?" said Jesus. *"Everything is possible for him who believes."*

Immediately the boy's father exclaimed, *"I do believe; help me overcome my unbelief!"* (Mark 9:23-24).

Isn't that a great response! The guy simply admits his doubts and asks God to help him. He just broke new ground with God! As the crowd ran to Jesus, Jesus rebuked the demon and drove him out. In fact, he commanded the demon to never come back to the boy again. When the demon left, the boy was so overcome with peace that he looked dead. People even said he was dead. But Jesus took his hand and helped him to his feet. He had been totally healed.

Later, the disciples were very interested in what just happened. They wanted to know why they couldn't drive the demon out. Jesus answer is startlingly simple, *"This kind can come out only by prayer"* (Mark 9:29).

They only come out by prayer: did I miss something? Somewhere in that account, did Jesus say to the group around him, "Let's pause, and pray so I can drive this demon out." Nope.

Jesus is not advocating a secret kind of prayer that drives out demons. He's not even suggesting there is a formula that can spook Satan. What he means is that prayer is his great secret to success. Prayer is the secret to his miracles:; prayer is the secret to his knowledge; prayer is the secret of his amazing power. And then he shows his disciples that prayer is his secret to defeating and driving out demons.

Jesus by his nature had authority over Satan. He never gave that up. But prayer gave him the direction from the father as to how to use his authority. He needed constant guidance from Heaven because he had made himself dependent on the Father in every way.

Here's the interesting thing: we know prayer is important. Jesus was on the mountain praying—getting direction from God, when he was transfigured. He didn't need to pause to pray some more, he was already in connection and communication with *the* Father. He took the spiritual discipline of prayer and moved it into his daily life.

Some are going to ask, so it's worth answering now, "Does that mean I can drive out demons?" Not for show. But if a demon is suddenly in front of you, foaming at the mouth, and the Father wants you to tell it to leave—you will be able to do exactly that. Prayer gives me the power to do anything God wants me to do. If God wants us to walk on water, we can. How do we know if God wants us to walk on water? Prayer!

As long as we see ourselves as servants of God, we are merely an extension that he is working through. It's not about us, our knowledge or our power, it's about who we are connected to. (Think vine and branches here.)

A *discouraging* word—anything you do for God will be opposed by Satan, the world, and your own flesh.

An *encouraging* word—no power on earth is stronger than the power of God. As long as you stay connected, he'll guide you through the satanic attack. When the enemy does come against you, the best weapon you have is the unlimited resources of God almighty. You just need to stay connected.

Jesus didn't have any sin-static in his connection with God. We must keep sin and worry out of the way so that we can maintain a strong connection.

Expect—God is Going to do New Things

A step forward in your walk with God is an open door to many more things. As you begin to pray more, you'll see more of what God is doing. This is just the beginning of your adventure.

After the Transfiguration, Jesus asked his disciples not to talk about what they had seen until after the resurrection. Mark 9 says the disciples obeyed Jesus, but discussed among themselves what "*rising from the dead*" meant (Mark 9:10). God had many more wonderful things planned and he wanted them to be a part of it.

God doesn't just want to do new things, he wants to involve you. But often, we first meet the idea of doing something new with resistance. Our church missions director, Eva, sat across from Jeremy, who was looking to start a new church in Palm Springs. Jeremy shared his heart and vision for the new church that would be called Movement West. We'd been praying for Jeremy for over two years, and now he was ready to ask our church to help him in his efforts. We could see God doing many miracles, even giving them possible property. Jeremy was ready to leave everything he'd built in another state and come start fresh in California.

Eva said, "Jeremy, I know this. I want to be on the inside of what God is doing, not the outside. The only thing I am interested in is if God is in this. I want to be working where God is."

I hope that's your prayer. Anywhere God is at work, that's ground you want to be on.

In his book, *Fire and Rain: The Wild-Hearted Faith of Elijah*, Ray Pritchard shared that after the 2004 tsunami disaster in Indonesia, his friend Ramesh Richard, a professor at Dallas Seminary, sent an e-mail with a one-sentence prayer. Ray said Ramesh called it a *dangerous* prayer. His prayer was simply this: "Lord, do things we're not used to."

As God does new things, you can joyfully join him, or complain that things aren't the way they used to be. I know this: after you've really seen God work—you're hooked. Those times that you can truly stand in awe of God gives life to your soul. Your inner being breathes fresh air when you truly feel you've been close to the workings of the Almighty.

God might call a new pastor to your church. You can sit and think about how he's not as good as the old pastor, or you can embrace him wholeheartedly and help him carry out God's vision in your church. He might bring a new member into your church family. You can welcome that new person and be thankful for God's direction, or begin seeing all their flaws and complain that they don't really belong. You can welcome them in, or treat them like outsiders. God might ask

Chapter 10—Building On New Ground

you to befriend someone new because he's at work in that person's life and wants you to get involved in what he is doing.

Amazing things will happen when you simply pray, "Lord, do things we're not used to."

Expect—Continued Groundbreaking

Breaking new ground with God isn't something you do once and it's finished—a relationship with God takes constant groundbreaking. Have you ever met a person who thinks God stopped doing God-stuff when Jesus ascended? Or someone that thinks God stopped doing miracles after the age of the apostles? God doesn't have any less strength now than he did long ago. He's still God, and he is still busy doing God-things. And he will continue to call mankind to new ground until that glorious day he comes again.

In describing the Transfiguration, Matthew uses a *passive* verb: *metamorphoo*. Why does *passive* matter? Because it means Jesus did not transfigure himself (he didn't hold his breath and push hard!), God the Father is behind transformation. Paul uses the same verb to describe spiritual transformation in believers when he writes:

> *Do not conform any longer to the pattern of this world, but be transformed* (**metamorphoo**) *by the renewing of your mind.*
>
> — Romans 12:2

The idea is that God does the transforming, but we must let him.

After Jesus was raised from the dead, John 21 describes an incredible incident. Peter and several other disciples were fishing. They hadn't caught anything when early in the morning a mysterious figure on the shore asked if they had caught any fish. He then instructed them to throw their net on the other side. When they did, the nets were swamped with fish. The Apostle John said to Peter, "*It is the Lord!*" In other words: we *know* who this is! We've seen this miracle before. This is Jesus stuff.

What happened next is very funny. Peter put on his cloths and jumped in the water. A friend suggested Peter thought he was going to walk on water. He was probably so excited he got disoriented and forgot he was in a boat. He reaches shore just in time to discover it is indeed Jesus who was speaking to him. Jesus tells him to go back and help the other disciples bring in the fish. So pretty much, jumping out of the boat was completely pointless. Jesus still sent him back!

What John records next is beautiful. Jesus invites his disciples to come and eat with him. Probably, one reason for this resurrection appearance is Jesus wants just a little more sweet time of fellowship with the men he loves so much.

By the way, as a side note, it is worth noting that the number of fish they caught, 153 (see John 21:11), was the same number of types of fish that were known to be in the sea of Galilee at that time. Many scholars think this is a visual form of the great commission. The sea represents the world, and in the world, is every kind of person God wants to reach. Or, John might have record the number of fish because he's the one who had to clean them, and thus he knew how many fish there were, and dog gone it, he was going to write it down.

After they ate, Jesus asked Peter, "*Do you love me?*" Peter responds that he does indeed love Jesus, but his word for love is not the same as Jesus'. Jesus is asking, do you *Agape* me. Agape is the strongest form of sacrificial love. Peter responds that he and Jesus are good—they're buddies. Jesus asks Peter three times, and all three times Peter gives the same response. Peter was wounded that Jesus would ask him three times. The message is obvious. Peter denied Jesus three times, so Jesus asks him three times about his love. Has it grown any? Has it changed? Has it deepened from that dark night when Peter hovered near another fire?

What's Jesus doing here? He's breaking new ground with Peter. And it hurts! Peter wasn't excited at that moment, he was frustrated with Jesus. But notice, Jesus still pressed on with his question—*Do you love me?* His failure a few nights earlier is something Peter would rather forget. It was his worst moment. His heart was exposed. His love was not complete and overflowing as he had promised it would be. He had acted out of self-preservation—he didn't know he'd ever see Jesus again.

Jesus is willing to hurt you to heal you. Just as ground is wounded to be broken open, so Christ must at times wound us to bring us to new ground with him.

The reason Jesus wounded Peter is because he wants to build on the new ground. Had Jesus' forgiven Peter? Yes. And it's demonstrated in Jesus perpetual command, "*Feed my sheep.*" Jesus is saying, "Peter, you're not out. *In fact, if you'll let me deal with this issue from your past, if we can get past this, then I have an incredible future for you. I want to use you greatly.*"

Chapter 10—Building On New Ground

For God to use you, you may need to deal with some past mistakes. You cannot drag the chains of your past as you try to follow Jesus. He goes where chains don't. It's like Jesus is telling Peter to take off the chains of his past so that they can build now on the new ground. For Peter, it was the sin of denying Jesus. For you it might be an affair, an immoral lifestyle, an abortion or something you said. You may have hurt another person, or perhaps, in your past you actually denied Jesus, and you're wondering if he can ever forgive you. And Jesus is saying, "Yes! Let's deal with this. Let's deal with the pain so that we can move forward."

Just as Jesus had a plan and a role for Peter in his kingdom, he has a plan and a role for you. God cannot have all of you until you let him have your past. That might require some time alone; some shed tears; a decision to never go back to old sins; to live in his mercy.

God Doesn't Play the Fair Game

At some point Jesus and Peter began walking down the shore. John trailed after them. After asking Peter three times "*do you love me?*" and telling him to "*feed my sheep*", Jesus then gave Peter an insight to the future.

> [W]hen you were younger, you dressed yourself and went wher you wanted; but when you are old, you will stretch out your hands, and someone else will dress you and lead you where you do not want to go.
>
> — John 21:18

With those words, Jesus is telling Peter that he is going to die. Peter had said he would be willing to die for Jesus, and now Jesus is revealing that is indeed Heaven's plan. Jesus even prefaces the statement with "*I tell you the truth.*" This is Heaven's truth—the Father in heaven has decreed this.

In exasperation to Jesus' question, "*Do you love me?*" Peter points to John who is following a few steps behind, "*What about him?*" Jesus answered, "*If I want, he could remain alive until I return.*" Wouldn't that have been amazing! Jesus did not say that was God's plan, just that if he wanted to, he could make it happen. He could cause John to skip death altogether and live until the Second Coming.

What Jesus told Peter about John is shocking. Both these men stood with Jesus at the transfiguration. Both had seen the glory of

Jesus. Yet, Jesus revealed they might have very different roles to play in the upcoming ministry.

Jesus then asked Peter, *"What is that to you?"* and demanded, *"You must follow me."*

From Peter's point of view, it probably did not seem fair. Church history tells us that Peter would die a terrible death. First, he would watch his wife executed, and then they would lay him down to be crucified. What about John? Jesus did not promise that John would not die. But, John's experience recorded in Revelation was certainly close to the Second Coming. Jesus was not asking Peter to *"follow me"* by walking in John's footsteps. Peter had to take a very personal path. Our walk with Jesus may involve suffering that others do not have to endure. Some may have to pay a higher price than others on this side of Heaven. Jesus, we discover, is not worried about being fair—he's focused on fulfilling our life purpose.

As you move forward with God, you will learn that he will ask you to do some things that don't seem fair. He will ask you to serve people you don't want to serve. He will tell you that you must forgive people that you don't think deserve to be forgiven. He will give you assignments you don't want.

Jesus did not say, "Follow your heart!" He never said, "Follow your dreams!" he said, *"Follow me."* In fact, leave all your dreams behind. Leave your will and your desires and your wants behind. They are probably the things that got you in trouble to begin with.

There are missionaries that God sends to the poorest regions of the world. There are missionaries who are murdered for their faith. And then, there are missionaries to Hawaii. Seem fair? That's because Jesus isn't worried about fair—he's making disciples. Jesus will tell you to help people that you don't want to help—people you think are taking advantage of the church. Yet, you obey him, not because it's fair, but because he's Lord.

As you move forward with Jesus, he wants you to simply trust him. He knows what's best for you. Everyone does not have the same future. We do not each have the same experience with Jesus. Each disciple is growing toward Jesus on a very personal walk, even as we walk together in the community of church. God knows how much money he's going to give you; what position he will assign you in the church; what people he wants you to help. If you're a pastor, he knows how big your church will be, and he knows how big Rick War-

Chapter 10—Building On New Ground

ren's church is. He's not worried about fair, not for one moment. Because fair is a hindrance to deep. You cannot go deeper with Jesus when you spend all your time looking at what God told others to do.

When I was a kid I loved the Bill Gaither trio. They were great. But then one of the members disappeared from the public, and the trio became the Bill Gaither vocal band. One member was noticeably absent—Danny Gaither. Why did Danny stop singing with the group? Because his voice broke and he was suddenly unable to sing the way he once had. He later returned to the Gathers—but not on stage under the lights. He began driving the tour bus. It probably didn't seem fair to him at first, but Danny said he learned to have joy in driving the bus because it was *very important*.

Expect—New Ground to Involve the Church

You cannot build on new ground spiritually and skip the importance of a local body of believers that you belong to—the church. The church is a vital part of your spiritual health.

Years ago, my grandfather built the house he would raise his family in. Along the front of the house, he built a big porch. In the evening, he and my grandmother would sit on the porch as the kids played in the yard and they would greet neighbors as they went by. There was a sense of community. Today, front porches are disappearing. We try not to engage with our neighbors. As a culture, we are losing our sense of community. Unfortunately, that is also true of the church. We are becoming so consumed by personal experience that we do not understand the importance of community to our walk with God.

Three times Jesus told Peter that the way to show the Lord that he loved him was to *feed* the sheep. Jesus is reminding Peter that he is a shepherd, and he has sheep. His sheep are his church. Love my church Peter. Take care of my church. The church is not the building (the sheep pin), the church is the people, the sheep.

This might have frustrated Peter. He might have thought, "Look, I said I love you, not that I love your sheep. Actually, some of your sheep really annoy me. The truth is, I don't love them. I love you. You're the one that I said I would follow." He didn't say that, of course. But it's very close to what many today would have said to Jesus. Often people will say, "I love Jesus, not the church."

If you love Jesus, but not the church, then your love for Jesus is not very deep. It's not—or shouldn't be—very hard to love Jesus. Jesus never sinned against you—ever. Jesus always behaved with love toward you. Jesus died for you. (Talk about unfair.) It's easy to love Jesus, and hard to love the church. Loving Jesus by loving the church is a greater test of our love than just loving Jesus. Your love is shallow if you only love those who love you. Jesus makes it clear—to love him is to love his people.

Jesus takes very personal how we treat his church. Remember when Jesus confronted Saul on the road to Damascus. Saul was on the way to persecute Christians. Jesus asked him, *"Saul, Saul, why do you persecute me?"* Now, Saul could have said, "What do you mean, we've never even met! I don't know you. I can't persecute you, because I've never even shaken your hand." But to Jesus, persecuting his people was the same as personally hurting him. Gossip in the church is to gossip against Jesus. To show unkindness, pride, or anger in the church is to treat Jesus that way. Jesus calls the sheep, *my sheep* (see John 21:15) and *my lambs* (see John 21:16). We are not just sheep and lambs; we belong to Jesus.

Here are a few ways that the church is a part of our spiritual growth and health:

1. The church puts us in circles we would not normally move in. It forces us to relate to and love people who are racially different than us. It demands we love people with a different political persuasion than our own. The church puts rich and poor next to one another on the same pew and in the same home group, so that even though they are economically different, they must love one another.

2. The church puts us near people less mature than ourselves. These are people we are to serve. They may be children who need to be taught in Sunday School, or other believers who are not as far along in their walk with God. By serving those who are less mature in Jesus, our own faith grows. Nothing will teach us the Bible like having to teach it to others.

3. The church puts us close to people more mature than ourselves. Not only are there people in the church we need to serve and to teach, there are some that we need to learn from. Both these groups will help us in our journey of breaking new ground with God.

4. The church will also put us on the path with some irritating people. (Read that again.) That's right, fellow believers sometimes drive one another crazy. There are probably some Christian's you don't even get along with; some other believers that, if you were really honest, you don't even like. But God has commanded you to love them, even though your personalities clash. These people teach us patience, love and empathy. God is using them also to help us break new ground with him. If we can't love them, then we can't love him.

Expect—To Give More

Each step we take toward God is a step away from ourselves. Each time we break new ground, we discover how much more we love God than we love our own self. As we mature and grow, our desire to give increases as well.

According to the Greek scholar Origen, Peter was ordered to die by emperor Nero. Peter himself requested not to die in the same manner Jesus did, and was subsequently crucified upside down. Add to that the fact that his wife was executed before him, and his suffering is unimaginable to most modern believers. He paid a heavy price for following Jesus.

Peter once said he would die for Jesus. He wasn't ready then to endure that suffering, as demonstrated by his denial of Jesus. On the seashore, as Jesus and Peter walked, Peter broke through to new ground spiritually. His love for Jesus did grow. And for the years to come, he would grow more and more in love with Jesus. Finally, his love would be tested anew, and this time he did not deny Jesus. In fact, standing on the firm ground of solid faith, Peter's faith did not waver.

As we come to the end of this book, would you make Jesus an offer? Would you say, "Jesus, you can have more of me."

I don't know how much Jesus will take. I know he won't be worried about it being fair. But this I do know—you can trust him. If you offer him more of yourself, and you really mean it, you can trust him to act only in love toward you. Wherever you are in your walk with God, you can make God that simple offer—Jesus, you can have more of me.

Make Room for God to Work

Breaking new ground with God requires we make room for God to work. That we keep our relationship with him invigorated. That we remove the barriers of sin and worry and keep our faith fresh. To break new ground with God forces you to ask the hard question—am I giving Jesus all?

Our church hosted singer Dallas Holmes for a concert a few years ago. He is well known for the song, *Rise Again*. At lunch Dallas offered to sit with our kids, but they were shy and wanted to sit with mommy.

I asked Dallas, "You sing the song *Rise Again* over and over. You go all over the country, and no matter how many new songs you write, people are going to want to hear you sing *Rise Again*. Does it ever lose its freshness?"

"Not as long as my relationship with Christ stays fresh and new," Dallas said.

By this he meant; we can do anything—even stay faithful to old things, or do new things—so long as our walk with God is healthy and vibrant.

As you move forward with God, this is not a solely spiritual activity. He is going to ask you to serve people, work in ministry and give deeply of yourself. As you give yourself fully to God, you are in for a lifetime of ground breaking experiences.

In Summary
If we want to Break New Ground with God:

- We must be very serious about prayer. Jesus became flesh and blood, and yet did amazing things because of his connection to the Father. We should not say we can't follow Jesus, because he *did* play by our rules.
- We cannot allow our personal sense of awe and wonder to fade.
- We should see the Second Coming as something we live toward, not just something we look forward to. A real belief in the Coming of Jesus would change how we behave now.
- We need to accept God's Word as truth, even if it is painful.
- We must decide to trust God with our worries and disappointments.
- We should believe that God will richly reward those who remain faithful.

Digging Deeper

1. In this chapter we looked at 5 things we can expect as we break new ground with God. Let's look a little more personally at those.

   Expect that the Devil is going to be in your face.
   - Have you experienced personal attack as you've sought to deepen your journey with the Lord?

     [ ] Yes   [ ] No

   Expect God is going to do new things.
   - What are some new things God has done during this season?

     _____
     _____

   Expect continued ground breaking.
   - Do you look forward to the next chapter in your walk with God?

     [ ] Yes   [ ] No

   - What are some areas where you hope to break new ground with God?

     _____
     _____
     _____

   Expect new ground to involve the church.
   - What are some ways your church family has strengthened your walk with God?

     _____
     _____
     _____

Chapter 10—Building On New Ground

Expect to give more.
- As we discussed this point, I suggested a really tough prayer, "Jesus, you can have more of me." How willing are you to make that offer to God?

    [ ] No way
    [ ] I'm working toward that, but I'm not there
    [ ] I wish I could truly pray that prayer
    [ ] I have some things to take care of before I can truly offer God more of me
    [ ] I'm scared, but I'm willing to offer God more of myself
    [ ] Yes! It's time I told God he can have more of me.

2. Write some things we should expect as we break new ground with God that are not list above.

    _____
    _____
    _____

3. Have you ever found yourself comparing your life circumstances to others and feeling God has not treated you fairly?

    [ ] Yes   [ ] No

    - Take a moment and write down some people in the Bible who might not have felt they were treated fair by life's turns.

    _____
    _____
    _____

4. What are some things you have personally discovered as you sought to break new ground with God?

   _____
   _____

   - What are some things that surprised you?

     _____
     _____

   - What new things did you discover about God?

     _____
     _____

   - What did you learn about yourself that you *did not* like?

     _____
     _____

   - What did you learn about yourself that you *did* like?

     _____
     _____

5. As you look at the road ahead with God, what scares you the most? That is important to consider, because our fears are indications of where we will need to walk by faith.

   _____
   _____
   _____

Chapter 10—Building On New Ground

6. Review the six truths and ask yourself if there has been any change since you started purposefully seeking to break new ground with God in this study.

    - How has your prayer life changed?

    _____
    _____

    - Do you have a greater sense of awe for God? What are some things you are doing to cultivate a personal sense of awe and wonder at God?

    _____
    _____

    - Has your anticipation of the Second Coming begun to change how you live daily? In what ways?

    _____
    _____

    - Have you begun reading the Bible any differently than you did before?

    _____
    _____

    - What are some specific worries and fears that you have chosen to trust to God's care during this season?

    _____
    _____

    - God's faithfulness in rewarding his servants affects our service to him now. Has your personal desire to serve him grown as you've thought about the richness of his rewards?
    I truly hope it has!

        [ ] Yes   [ ] No